JUSTO JORGE PADRÓN • MEMORY OF THE FIRE

JUSTO JORGE PADRÓN

Memory of the Fire

SELECTED POEMS
1989–2000

Translated from Spanish by
Louis Bourne

ANVIL PRESS POETRY

Published in 2004
by Anvil Press Poetry Ltd
Neptune House 70 Royal Hill London SE10 8RF
www.anvilpresspoetry.com

This book is published with financial assistance
from The Arts Council of England

Designed and set in Monotype Bell by Anvil
Printed and bound in England
by Cromwell Press, Trowbridge, Wiltshire

ISBN 0 85646 346 9

A catalogue record for this book
is available from the British Library

ACKNOWLEDGEMENTS

'Behind the Locked Door' originally appeared in *Outposts Poetry
Quarterly*; 'The Hand That Writes You', 'Like a White-Hot Loom'
and 'Mount Lentiscal' in *Contemporary Poetry from the Canary
Islands* (London: Forest Books, 1992); 'The Choice' in *Poetry
Review*; 'Text for an Angel' and 'Legend of a River' in *The Bitter
Oleander*; 'Weeds of Desire' in *Illuminations*. The first stanza of
'The Hand That Writes You' also appeared engraved in black
granite in Spanish and English at the New Lines exhibition
at the Millennium Dome in North Greenwich.

All translations are based on the texts in *Memoria del fuego:
Obra poetica 1965–2000* ('Memory of the Fire: Collected Poems
1965–2000'), Barcelona: Lumen, 2000.

Contents

From SKETCHES IN A PARENTHESIS
(Poems Not Included in Books)
Trazos en un paréntesis
(Poemas no recogidos en libros)
1965–2000 (2000)

PREFACE

JUSTO JORGE PADRÓN's collected poems in Spanish, which
have the same title as this English selection, now consist of
twenty books. His first anthology in English, *On the Cutting
Edge* (London: Forest Books, 1988), contained poems from
eight books, including a largely different selection from *Only
the Hand that Writes You Dies*, a book that was published a year
after *On the Cutting Edge* appeared. This second anthology
presents poems from the 1989 work as well as from twelve
other books published since then – one of which, *Writ in Water*,
was completed in 1966 though not published until 1996.

Justo Jorge Padrón was born in the city of Las Palmas,
Grand Canary Island, in 1943. He studied law, philosophy and
Spanish literature at Barcelona University and later extended
his studies in Paris and Stockholm. For eight years he main-
tained a legal practice until he gave it up to devote himself
entirely to literature. To poetry he brings the lawyer's pursuit
of the precise word coupled with the wide experience of a
translator in dealing with different sensibilities and poetic
styles. Padrón lived in Sweden for several years, won a number
of prizes for his translations into Spanish of Scandinavian
poetry (including the international awards of the Swedish
Academy and the National Institute of Norwegian Culture),
and, according to Swedish Academy member Artur Lundkvist,
established himself as 'the essential mediator between Nordic
and Spanish literatures'.

A word about prosody: free verse in Spanish, especially in
Spain, is often not free. Most poets, including Padrón, write in
hendecasyllabic lines, varying these with others of seven, nine
and fourteen syllables, for the eleven-syllable line has some-
thing like the tradition and musicality of the iambic penta-
meter in English poetry, while the other lines maintain the
rhythm and offer dramatic variety. Part of Padrón's art is his
dedication to the music of his verses. He has written that
'Poetry should attempt a magic balance between persuasion,
mystery and suggestion'.

Apart from his awards for specific works, Justo Jorge Padrón has won numerous international distinctions, among them the European Prize for Literature (Belgrade, 1986), the International Grand Prize for Literature (Bulgaria, 1988), the Golden Wreath of the Struga International Poetry Festival (Yugoslavia, 1990), the Blaise Cendrars Award of the Swiss International Poetry Festival (Yverdon and Neuchâtel, 1994), the International Poetry Prize (Trieste, Italy, 1999), an Honorary Doctorate from Ricardo Palma University in Lima, Peru (2001) and the Leopold Sedar Senghor Grand Prize for Poetry (Senegal, 2003). He is one of the most widely translated living poets in the Spanish language. The following selection presents the English-speaking reader with an ample choice from the Spanish poet's work, which is marked by a rich variety of moods, constituting a lasting legacy of poetic experience.

LOUIS BOURNE
Madrid, July, 2003

NOTE

Dates of books in the Contents and on section title pages give the publication year of a book in brackets, e.g. (1998). For the first collection, *Writ in Water*, and the final four, from *The Fire in the Diamond* onwards, dates of composition are also given, without brackets. These four books were first published in *Memoria del fuego: Obra poetica 1965–2000* ('Memory of the Fire: Collected Poems 1965–2000'), Barcelona: Lumen, 2000.

from

Writ in Water

Escrito en el agua

1966 (1996)

Unconquerable Love

As you asked me, you half-shut your eyes
with your doubts about love. When seeing that bonfire
raised by your pupils, I suddenly knew.
Something gleamed in the stars, was reflected in your
    body,
and there, glowing and heady from the full moon,
free, with the woodland fragrance of myrtle
I went on living your skin, crossing the limits
of that moistened kingdom craving me
beneath night's earthy grandeur.

I knotted with you till I rose to the heaven
of fireflies, listening to the glassy
song of crickets and the deep breathing
of your round breasts attracting time.

Gazing at you naked beneath the sun of hands,
knowing you unconquerable in memory,
falling in the agony of kisses
I thrust into your shadow of trees and centuries,
veined with genesis, into you, chalice of dawn,
little church in which to pray to God,
faithful ivy, so intimate and celestial,
ivy reading me words of the rain
beneath wakes and stars of a shining cosmos.

A Proud Broken Dream

There, too, your lightning face remains,
a deep blaze blinding all,
a caressing sandbank on which arrives
my proud broken dream fragmented with foam.

From then on, you've been an oasis of memory,
my secret lamp, delirium's jewel
unfolding its phosphorescent light
in the country with no destination of my wandering.

Now that we are no more beneath the sun
of that fascinating idolatry,
and the slow misery of years
has been darkening our bodies
with punishment's dismal ash,
I still keep asking
if your lips harbour that smooth fever
that always throbbed in our kiss,
and if you still hoard the fire of nights
when we devoured each other in our gaze,
feeling the world's heartbeat in our embrace
and that unconquerable love of the gods we were.

Writ in Water

Homage to John Keats

What I write in water is at once erased,
but if, in water, I place the fervour of your name,
the air dreams of being woodland music
where the heart beats with what sings
hidden and is never expressed. The stealthy
radiant presences of nymphs appear
dancing in the shade, and the half-dreamed forest,
standing, wakened by your word's light,
turns into frozen shining life
that you alone set amidst the beautiful,
in the flowing soul of all that lasts
and in that young death that spoke with your voice:
'Beauty is truth – that is all
ye know on earth, and all ye need to know.'
Your solitary name remains writ in water.
The years and waves shall never erase it,
nor fire, breeze, nor oblivion.

Night of the Invisible

The ear listened to the world's abyss,
the murmur of absence, its deep vibration,
a spiral climbing from the tired body
to bring news of the lost and the eternal.
Awake in the night dew, it captured night's
scattered signals: the distance of dogs,
shameless dragonflies of rain or wind,
a distant car whose death-rattle dies out,
and then that silence following
the squawk of a bird astray in anguish,
wandering on the last horizon.
The lost sounds turn
into shadows or legends of snaking ghosts,
something muddled seething in memory.
Night and its mystery empty out.
Are they dreams, perhaps, that can't return?
The dogged music of distant deliriums?
A cascade of insinuating waves
reaches and reveals me. Whose is the voice?
From what place and time? How can I hear it?
I foresee its disquiet, its frightened howl.
But something gives, releases the ropes.
Everything's pulling away, the struggle, gloom,
the cry calling me in the void,
and slowly the dream invades the dark,
soothing fear's stealthy sounds.

Your Life Is Ours

In my childhood nights they told me,
among the boldest of our ancestors,
there are some who come back to feel,
within our blood, the existence
death robbed them of. This event
would explain the course of contradictions,
or those lonely illumined successes
I sense I shared with the stealthy
echoes throbbing in my veins.

I don't believe your life is only yours,
nor mine solely mine.
In them shines the Viking's sail heading for the fjord.
The brave warrior falls, dying for his honour.
The Bedouin's prayer thrills the stars.
We heard the hetaira's hushed agony.
Children, generations with helplessness and faith.

All we were and forgot
pierces memory once more
with the centuries and arid plains of earth.
Your life's a key half-opening an unknown sea.
Take care of it. It belongs equally to us all.

from

Only the Hand
That Writes You Dies

Sólo muere la mano que te escribe

(1989)

The Hand That Writes You

They are not history, dates, the hours we embrace,
not even a handful of words
or flocks of images in eloquent air.
From my forehead springs your name's flow,
and in that still water staring at you
from the past, you live always just as you are,
unburnt by the years.

I sketch your snowy profile, signs
dictated to me by winter with its bleak truth.
White laughter, birches, slow fascination,
time without time, days in night,
sun going back to its wellspring of aromas
beside the cabin's tamed fire.

The world dissolves in your gaze,
the page longing to keep you
in an eternity that aches and stays.

Only the hand that writes you dies.

In the Abyss of My Body

In the glass goblet, wine glistens,
dances with a fire's enigma.
Is its secret a song or whisper?
I go on amid the dark of my most quivering half
where death exhales her greed.
I feel her face go by, her sphinx presence
tying and untying a grim knot.
I imagine her eyelids now descend to my forehead.
Who forces me, thrusting me outside myself?
My body's night fills me with fear.
Answer me, skin, you who listen
to my blood's abrupt language,
and feel as no one else its humours and entrails
bringing me news of my marrows' abyss.
Discover me with no fear. What organ conspires,
what infiltrating enemy awaits our dream?
Nothing can you do in your labour
except only contain its élan.
Every day I look at you in the mirror
like a wave threatening amid transparence.
Is it true I was born to be a voice?
Tell me, why do I sing, why do you teach me?
Faithful torrent devoured in your fleeting trace.
Wipe out the ravenous images plaguing me,
live with me, beloved sensation,
so morning can open its doors
in you, my word, adventurous body.

The Poet

Look at this man ignored, that one scorned
for his word's essential gift.

He who loves beauty as well as freedom
as both are the force of his fire.

He who rebels against unjust power
by exercising his grave discord.

He who lights up the word 'sun'
when he writes it, and when he says 'bird',
air is a gust singing in the brush.

He who polishes his verse to the nth degree
like tempered steel to defend the life
of all that pulses, grows, flies and dreams.

He who listens to worlds far from his own
and, absorbed, extends for us a new space.

He who breaks the traps of sorrow
and the lock of all stagnant water
to go deep, lucid, into its dark plain.

That same fellow who one day opens a chink
towards death in order never to be
a pebble trapped in the wall of hate.

The Hallucinating Tundra

The gaze outstretched into the tundra's
white desert. Perpetual motionless trail
where ink etches the traces of darkness.

Invisible falcons tear at the silence.
Their crystal names run through me,
swirls of winter cloud them with delirium.

It's still night for those who dream.
Unexpectedly the dunes open their white eyelids.
I waylay the whispers springing from their ice.

Why do you want to die in my unremembering?
You who still scour it with a tender shudder,
come out of the mind, draw near my fire
so I can give wings to your flight,
voice to your signs, song to your light.

The Seething Setting

From my desk, a sheet of paper glides
onto the floor. I gently try to lift it
and I feel a syllable bite.
Unbelieving, I watch it, flatten my look
level with its whiteness, and a chimeric
wave leaps towards my eyes. A sailboat's bow
makes horizons grow and the green words
seethe, hopping over every line.

With the gulls fly swift dives
of dolphins. Horses' hooves
thunder on the stones. Their stormy manes
the wind's flags. I don't know why
the gypsies' violins quarrel now.
Why do you want to know which is my dream?
Barely to halt the weight of rain
with the open palms of my hands
or with my body in flight while my eyes laugh.

The gull, unharmed, divided
the sheet of dawn into two equal halves.
This summer day is so alive.
The dog grows furious barking at the waves.
See how the bees celebrate their work?
The grass now returns to the mountain with the rain.
No, this day's not mine,
perhaps it's the past of a fuller future.
An oboe's quivering
is sketched in the aura of this line.
When I close my eyes, I reach the stars.
Yes, I'm a thorn claiming its rose.

The light trembles in puddles,
thrills with human tenderness,
rises, stretches in my ears.

I feel the shiver of syllables being born,
flowing from a chute of indigo planets.
The clock counts in detail
the songs left the sparrow.
I want to write beyond inebriation,
write on a world tearing down limits
to calm the thirst of the universe.
A poem's freshness lasts longer
than the high loneliness of the pyramids.

She went and left old age in my body.
But where can that woman of mist be,
the wine that sang in our mouths,
that fullness that fled in a lightning flash,
leaving a tremor of wings in my blood?
Ah, happiness, are you by chance
the unending smile, the country of dew?
Ask your wound why it never forgets me.
Suddenly an aroma reminds me
of every dimension of what I've lost.

Who'll search her cold for her threat of love?
Every heartbeat pricks the blood that feels it,
that patient, unexplainable ember
still used by love to summon its chimera.
Let knights in lake armour, on rolling
horses, spring up from the rivers:
they must look after our lineage.

My heart, scarcely a joyful beggar,
needs only a filament of love.

Beloved enemies, is my silence enough?
Who says I'm not the bard from Atlantis?
Who crowned the dawn with anointed words?

O poets, thieves of mystery.
Through my blue notebook of verses
passed a comet's timid fragrance
with a feathery secret in its pupils.
Every day the archer aims precisely
there where the pain will be strongest.

Through a margin of error, night falls
in this hour's surprised thirst
and its blazes bite the moss of paper,
this white sandstone, till the water hears
and hurriedly drowns it, invites it to shipwreck.
Behind each laugh, death's
tormented eye is detected.
Our poor words are the shades
of the forgotten corpse we shall be.
When the sea hides us, we are the very waves.
Hope is the tear postponed of man.

Poem, only to you belongs
all I have left to live.
To live is to choose between submission
to what we were bequeathed or the painful
search for our still unwritten traces.
What harsh, choking uncertainty
to go on between inertia and the impossible.
Shall we be, beneath dying stars,
an oblivion that never wakes?
Visions casting my eyes into the distance,
come with my nostalgias turned to pulp and truth.

From space, that glitter of pollen
was born to lend me existence.
I was a boy living in the land of light.
My father's hand was the world beginning.
Four stones and the sea, my childhood kingdom.

When I was young, they called me wellspring.
Today I am just the lost syllable of the dark.
Love: an ocean of tenderness
with a few shining fish.
Starry stupor, you're the south!
The tree of space was spinning in its branches
the secret music of all the universe.

Tremulous writing wakes up
beneath the gold murmuring of the lamp.
The half-light is a disconsolate god
dreaming since he waits for the triumph of life.
The butterfly alighted on my forehead,
not knowing he gave me the enigma of a world,
premonitions of this god and his punishment:

alone from being a seed in the desert.

Text for an Angel

Once I wrote a text for an angel.
An invisible poem similar to his wings.
I still have no idea who'll fly better.
On I-don't-know-what occasions he remembers me
and at times, when I'm asleep, leaves on my lips
snowy melon pulp or releases in my ear
rippling arpeggios I'd never heard,
or he whispers remote, trembling words
that, with their keys, open the windows of water,
lanterned lights of a country beyond the shadows.
He leads me surely in his cosmic hand
through all the spaces dreamed by books,
and at the same time I am the youth
and eyes of all that lives
in the brotherly heartbeat of the breeze.
I feel the shiver of flowers making love,
the weeping of a star drowned in a puddle.
My invisible poem is my secret
and though I now proclaim and share it,
he, with his clear wings, in a trace of light
will insert oblivion in your smiles.

Captive of a Fixed Idea

I hear the paper drinking the sap of signs,
I open up harsh, obsessive words,
imprisoned by white walls
discovering my scorched days,
forbidden pulsings in the poem.

I am captive of a fixed idea
like the dogged clapper in its bell.
In my breathing, always those faint lines
and the dark presence of a snowy silence.

At times the metaphor resurges
from the depths of a garden with a handful
of fires in its hand or breaks its emotion
against harsh lightning hurrying to its exile.

The sea is my adventure, the birch my blaze,
love a short-lived season
exchanging its mirror for ashes
when revealing the face I cannot find.

But to be exact, I am night
rising to unending clarities
like a violin burning in the air that loves it.

The Name You One Day Want to Give Me

I must be the name you one day want to give me,
the value my poems may merit,
this dark substance circling in your pupils
till you decide to annul it.

In what secret night, with what sorrowful
delirious abandon, must you question me?

I can only offer you a handful of doubts,
slight forebodings, but I can go with you,
take you to the threshold of your dreams
so in them you can rewrite
fragments of your life and I be your reader,
with my selfsame word listening to you.

To Live

I reach no other unrest than that of looking
for words of existence, the ink discovering
doubt and glitter, the shaft of its mine.

To live is to share, loving what's not yet extinct.
To tempt appearances with a blind man's obsession.
In other words: to hear, to look directly
at the silence going by with sorrow and density,
sculpting in verses glass and its caress,
the time of what's human, the world's desire.

From love to death there's only one frontier,
an instant, that of air devouring us,
as if fire's enigma had gone by
and suddenly calmed the hollow of its absence
in the earth that never forgets us.

Like a White-Hot Loom

The stars spoke to me in my enigmas:
what frenzies of glass, what bitter substances
stay hushed in your unfinished corners?
This quiet fills with unease
for the world's thirst fits between my ears.
Disturbed, I ask, facing the vastness:
what strange forgetting could've given me birth?
I can only believe in this weird work
of signs and words making the sea dream,
for it's a magnet, an electric charge
springing from silence with seething song.
Only the poet knows how to speak to us of time's
mirror, of the enigma of metamorphoses
in the melting of its giddy mercuries,
and he alone can reveal us deep reality.
But listen to night arise in the conspiracy
of all the secrets still unuttered.
Feel how near the distant falls silent,
for the light you don't see is the shadow
watching with the cruelty of a choking soul.
You emerge, scathing night, like a white-hot loom
spitting signs, magma of a great alphabet
whose volcano bursts into mystery,
cleaving its roots into Cambrian waters.
You create the origin of space and its limits,
vestiges and rumblings, lacerated reliefs
leaving us their traces in the word
carved to be the flower of the look,
a roving calligraphy of limpid strokes
capturing the bold music of ideas.
And for you to exist, you must be the essential
between the trance of being and being it no more,

so you're the stone on which the cosmos rests,
for you're the cosmos and its first wellspring.
Night, lightning's shattering pride,
from your eyelids you spring with hushed fury
to give me news of blue unities,
dreams, cosmogonies of your name.
Rise up from muteness furiously free
like a watery bell on the cliffs.
Your look grasps me like a tiger of fever.
I rebel and cry to you with a gulf of tenderness.
Light me in your fire till I am flame
on your fragrant shore, in your dark dew.
Send down your ladder of starry glitter
so your shadowy sails, your whirling of winds,
can sail irrepressibly in my blood,
you, everlasting night, sparkling word,
perverse interruption of death.

from

Heard Faces

Los rostros escuchados

(1989)

Those Women

Who loved me so offered me their eyes.
Like oysters I gulp them down on this plate of smoke
brought by my inconclusive forgetfulness.
Inside they'll travel my body's chasms
and narrow passes, mirroring in streams of veins
landscapes that existed in all their secrets.
I don't know the currents, a dizzy chance
that must go with them on their ocean route,
but they'll be, in a unfailing way,
the simple, reduced matter we understand.

Such is the life of love, its fate:
to interpret breath, the sea throbbing
and oozing in the soul's thrilled force
to become barely excrement.

Hell's Lie

Don't believe the hell they fan in your eyes.
There'll be no rites of martyrdom there,
nor Lucifers of elegance,
no Majorcan Drach caves, no waters of boiling tar.
It must be like being amongst family
with the same quarrels and rebuffs.
Intimate enemies will stick to your side,
besieging your existence with envy.
Neither will those three or five distraught
women be lacking whom you uselessly loved.
Without your noticing, they exchanged the glow
of desire for this never-ending desert
having, as you still do, vitality,
unrepeatable life with a scorn for myth.
No, don't believe in that carnival of shadows,
for it's only unhappy memory's echo,
or perhaps the dogged, deserved cold
from wasting your decisive years in wanting
to perpetuate yourself in what you most loved.

The Winter of Death

To Rolando Certa, in memoriam

Like black syllables fallen into the mire,
lost and locked in their most sordid echoes,
with an odour of coldness and dripping
poverty, my memory turns mute.
Like a curtain collapsing,
probing stiff, mournful substances,
ringed by humiliated forces,
a rigour, a light, a frontal anguish
with its fist and vehemence nag me to tears
for the huge sum of an invulnerable hate.
Decayed masks of desire, moist,
come loose from the night,
the wounded laughs, their swift ichthyic scales,
the poisoned rite of rage.
I breathe, in the air, the taut curse,
its empire of ashes, its trail and helplessness.
Beneath a chorus of hounding deaths,
I see the long winter, dark stony trains,
a steep stairway going down
in a lost coffin towards the mist,
and I listen in the distance to a grieving silence.

The Choice

To Rafael Alberti, in memoriam

With a group of unknown shadows,
I headed for the big warehouse of bodies,
carrying out the order to be born.
There was such a rush, so many people.
I searched for a head that would be good
for my dreams, and said, 'Something romantic,
but with a touch of budding irony
and a pair of believing eyes in which life looms
with its clamour and fire. Can one sign up
for a size larger than one metre eighty?
But if they let me suit my fancy,
I'd ask for some hands, artist's hands,
delicate, subtle but strong,
to make all they embrace dream.
How delighted I'd be with a mystery voice,
one to gather murmur and flight,
the enigma of autumn hours,
yes, a sincere voice from a welcoming house
like a punctual, generous river
in the friendship or love it finds.
I know I've no time left to pick
the great intelligence or will
I'd have wanted, but leave me at least,
though the last thing, that imagination
flashing on the ceiling with the light in this room.'

Behind the Locked Door

I had forgotten that old door at home.
Its locked presence breathed
with the heartbeat of a strange guest.
I didn't dare open or even touch it.
I listened closely to its frail breathing,
the life it could have behind it,
the constant questions worrying me at times.
Gradually more disturbing, night drew on.
I forgot the rhythmic murmurings
filtered by its cold lintel.
I drew near, put my eye to the blue lock
and saw a girl holding oranges
in her hands. She tossed them into the air
and they kept turning into celestial comets.
Suddenly the suns began to wheel
from white to yellow, from rose to south,
vibrating their fertile hum in space.
The girl with the braids smiled,
went on smiling in her swing
beneath a cloak of centuries and stars.
'Who are you? Who?' I ventured to ask.
And the door began to melt away.
Her faint voice barely reached me.
'I am just a dream, a slight dream of yours
forgetting you for writing it.'

Mount Lentiscal

To my parents

I recognize you, my stones and grasses,
in the rash heart of summer.
Young earth of dreams,
peaceful volcano where birds are born.
Between us shines a vehement pact,
unspoken passion for our lineage.

It's your barest light that unfolds the morning
to the fiery enigma ripening dragon trees.
Your lithe geometry raises a temple in my eyes,
a calm of branches where sun can drink.
With its mist of stars, a dizziness looms
from the high railing of pines
and claws the universe with cascades of birds.

Dawn of tenderness, you spill onto clay soil
weightless squadrons of eucalyptus.
No lip forsakes the canticles of air.
Everything is vision present, nothing now imagined.
Bright unfolded fascinations,
tactile embodiment, dense masts and spars,
circular aromas crying out their colours
in the fertile thickness of world and matter.

I want to breed more trees, plough the sea of sky,
go on planting words with the trembling of grassblade,
setting up lamps and myths,
the silent love that swathes me.
In its happy waters, in breezes of a thousand shadows,
noon emerges with a diamond cry.
It's plenitude, the eye's pupil, a pulsing of ecstasy.

How long, tell me, can we hold
our living presence in the oneness of day?

I look for your primal intensity
in childhood's broadest fragrance.
To the cleanest clarity that I was
I link your lasting, vibrant duration.
Here dreams the house where a forest forms;
in it sleep little aerolites
entombed by unknown millennia
amidst volcanic gravel, crunching jet.

Beneath vine stock the wine hears new leaves
playing in the mirror of the fleeting.
Honey's migrations rouse
their wake of sleepwalking engines.
The bougainvillea crosses the whitewash light,
in the branches blaze its red butterflies.

The wind's horse travels your confines
with a swish of petals and whispers of flute,
gallops, pruning lilies with insane scissors,
and later lingers and sleeps in the vines
with its warm breath sketched on the grapes.
I'll never get used to death.
I want to go on pulsing in the summer.

In your dark pebbles my story unravelled.
In what longing for stars, in what hissing of pines,
in what yearning for flights and foamy horizons,
does my soul still sail? From the zenith of the mount,
the distant sailboats were like
the sunset's red rivers to the gaze,
setting out for regions of dew.

That melancholy hurts me in remembrance.
I still see it wheeling among the trees.
The wind and its idleness, the mesh of fallen leaves
engraving an undefinable sorrow,
a sphere of sounds and embers,
of reflections fading beneath their own shadows,
savage boy, deluded and alone,
watching time and its mystery stay awake,
almost without understanding, loving to delirium
nature's proud language
where everything greedily happens.

As though I'd never left your breath,
as though I'd never stopped arriving
with a more awkward boy in the pupils of my eyes,
today I go back to your primitive ring.
The sun's memory spreads out the paths.
Each stone, leaf or stem names your friendly face.

I am approached and ringed by a choir of flights.
In its warbling, down comes your caress
and in all you welcome, you rest and remain.

Oasis of volcanoes, refuge, earth of mine,
in your eyes I am reborn. You are steady strength
and time ripening my human lot.

Memory of an Aroma

Night half-opened dark syllables
in the brief silences of birds.
I left the edge of the road behind
to hear the earth's woodland heart.
Invisible presences slipped through
the dense air, a drift of resins.
I remained alert, deciphering
the echo of the leaves, that warm thickness
begun by a whisper of myrtle.
Just barely a breath, a distant trace,
an impulse that was astrolabe and flag,
wild in the honey of half-shadow.
But it wasn't thyme's steely freshness,
nor the cherry tree's blizzard bonfire
or the sensuality of magnolia and rose.
I shut my eyes to smell enigmas
that made me heady from the mist.
Its stars arrived with a seething of crystals,
fireflies from the sky, so sinuous and alive,
the swaying of submerged pines,
the passion of ascending names.
All language hearing the intact melody
rooting its unease in memory.
I sense a weight of thirsty branches,
a bubbling or the clean slipping
of some thighs weaving in the grass.
Now the moon catches fire from their bodies
as if a bright brush erased them
and that fragrance demolishes my burnt-out youth,
doggedly abolished by the years.

Weeds of Desire

A vast beach, as blonde
as Nausicaä's locks
that welcomed the sea's fury.
Yet it wasn't that sparkling sand
but her body, her naked body
imprisoning the September sky.
An indolent panther surprised
in sulphur's nocturnal bonfire.
And I went down to be tattooed in her,
to take hold of that rapture of stars
in the deep quartz of her eyes.
That's how her beauty was, digging its nest.
Awful amber that fire of her arms.
A red cascade of mine where strength sings
and the world's passion untwists
turning round her legs, round her vegetation
of rains and columns and blackest violets
over a crater melting in the mist.
And I could add that this vision advances
to reach the destructive breach
lit in the weeds of desire.

The Dogged Silence

From that modest, limited ambience
and its closed, readable walls,
perhaps we remember diffuse images:
the monotonous November rain
scratching the cloudy windowpanes,
the dogged silence of a city without cars,
or the refrigerator's irregular rumble
in our bodies' sluggish delight.
It's possible that now those old words,
to save us from ourselves,
come back with a tiny gleam
to wipe out the bitterness of this wound
deliriously revolving from its own inertia.

from

The Radiance of Hate

Resplandor del odio

(1993)

Dark Force

You are, hate, the tumult
flooding the eyes,
the inheritance of years,
the rancour of a life
stalking in its desert.

I hear the perpetual echo,
sleepless and thundering
against the harsh cracks
of locked doors.

Outside and here within,
once more the whirlwind rises –
a red sun torn –
on this frozen rock
closing in and choking me.

On your cold edge
and in my bitter
memory's steely light,
each instant hones you.

You come down soundless
in your spiderweb
and dirty what you dream,
pervert and curse it,
plunging into
blind, terrified days.

Never, never go away.
Protect me in your wrath,
only in you, dark force,

do I find the handhold
so as not to collapse,
never to give up
facing lifeless pain.

Only in you, my strength,
do I free myself from fear
by sucking your bitterness,
by invading the shadows,
only in you do I foresee
an invulnerable end.

It's That Black Drop

It's that black drop
monotonously falling,
subtly insisting
on a fixed thought's
damaged point.

All-embracing invocation
never unravelling
but gushing, stirring
on its longest night's
steely edge.

It incites with a piercing
stench and, from foam's
blindest cave,
blazing in its halo, grows
the wicked substance.

Persistent usury
oozing the scorn
of feeling shackled,
undoubtedly abhorred
by what it perhaps could
have loved without limits.

He's ringed by the desolate
world always hostile,
wounded by a sea,
gigantic and terrible,
throbbing and spreading

in that black drop
monotonously falling,
insisting on a strict
corner of memory.

The Ice of Your Name

Rain matter sombrely swirls.
Fed up in the moisture, I tear down dreams,
search in their remains for what my hand hushed.

I live in destruction, replacing
unbelievable protective measures
with a laborious lurking in the wrinkle of cold.

A boatman derelict on lifeless expanses,
I take to extremes remoteness boiling inside
with its black roots and blood spider.

I listen to myself in the night, prisoner
beside a fury subjected
to the strange stillness of this house of mist.

I slip in my inert memory's
rubble-filled basements with marine voices
climbing the ember of an abyss.

I line up my ravenous vertigos.
Lonely space does not understand,
cannot, the ice of your name.

Pyromaniac

I want to lock him in a chest of shadows,
cut his eagle's talons, the blinding flight,
the inquisitor flame lying in wait for me.
Ebony sun throbbing in every corner,
killing with jibes a senseless silence.

I hear his heart in the spite,
drinking in the torrent of anguish,
stirring up poisonous surges of surf
with the hammer of his invincible thunder.

I follow him and he convinces,
scorching me with his plea,
growing tight in my skin,
glittering in my blood.
He puts a tiger in my eyes,
and we are a claw,
the wildest will of the blaze.

Giant

They snatched his strength and impetus,
also his sullen gaze, the mist of his spirit,
the despair, rival of the ocean.

They harassed his space, divesting him
of his den, making him prisoner,
nailing him to a tree like a quivering arrow.

They covered him with jeering and there, in early morning,
abandoned him, broken, to his luck.

But they don't know hate grows in hurt
and reaches its invisible span,
its enraged giant's wrath,
when they leave him alone to his fate.

Creed

I believe in almighty hate,
creator of its shadow and its own threat.
I believe in the hairy beast breaking its chains
to make us crueller than tyrants themselves.

It was born from our parents, pain and fury,
grew amidst misery's latent injustice
and suffered torment beneath a pious egotism,
listening in the blood to its hangman's blows.

Here it lives to the right, to the left
of all rebels who scoff
at those still trusting in miracles.

I sense its word with the holy scorn
that lethally enthrones it in consciousness
facing the fear of an order wanting to bury it.

I celebrate it in the sleepless night,
heeding the pleas of grief,
and in the unanimous complaint of lost causes.

It is pure, unbeatable as desert light,
with its appalling presence in delirium.

I believe in the No of hate wanting to desecrate
the world, to destroy and raise it up
new from its cold ashes.

And from here it will come to be perpetuated,
while the life of men lasts,
with that overwhelming indignation
upholding the rancour that affirms us.

Our Father

I

Our father which art in this world,
hallowed be thy name and thy integrity,
may thy power avenge us so that thou fully rulest
and radiantly spurrest on to abomination
that floods the flames and their seas,
so we manage to reduce,
with thy sacred, avenging strength,
that man we designate as enemy.

II

Our father which doth harm and sharest thirst,
give us thyself today so thou mayest never reward
nor pardon the vile fellow, the false offender,
and neither let us fall
beneath merciful temptation,
nor may we forget to fulfill the opportune moment
of our faithful vengeance in the strict time
we may live on this earth.

Litany

Clean hate with no interferences,
like sea soaring over the shoal.
Hate staring at itself in the glass of wine,
seeing its blood rising in cut crystal's
fiery dance. Gaunt hate,
tight in the teeth, in feverish eyes,
with the shiver oozing from marrows,
carefully drinking itself.
The most luxurious hate, one that calmly
prepares its vengeance as if it were a canvas
and adorns details with the invisible stroke
of rare perfection summing up all.
Perfumed hate of the hetaira
who filters her slow-acting poison
in your body's veined garden.
Powerful manly hate with no concessions,
murdering with a lightning slash,
and that other sickly hate, cowardly, unsure,
hiding, scratching, choking on itself.
Abandoned hate, poor hate,
possesses only that alms
to keep its existence warm.
Hate of the mirror repeating
and copying its steady duality
of well-groomed cold in rancour.
Hate of surfeit, prepotent and greasy,
with its rabid calm, its bloated tedium.
Passionate hate burning in the mind
with a devouring fire devastating the corners,
the peace of memory. Subtle, polite hate,
like a cowardly soul's lethal fragrance.

Desert hate, so frugal and Bedouin,
so scorpion, green and resistent.
Self-absorbed hate, locked in its obelisk
like a finger of shadow pointing to God.
Genocide hate tolling in the night
with the sober clapper spreading death
towards every core of the planet.

Here

Here on the rock burned by the surf,
I hate the light, the air, the faces I kissed,
love buried in its ashes.

Here facing the whips of wind,
free and determined, I listen only to the void's
thick rancour, its worn scepticism,
so like this body suffering its gloom.

Here, the frenzy of the broken answer.
I shout to this sea that tears pain,
sinking, smashing it in its sheer pride.

Here, facing myself and all my life,
without pity or redeeming hope,
with the blind incapacity to scorch the sky.

Here on the rock forgotten by the surf.

The Odour of Lust

It's wonderful that hate
has the odour of lust,
greedy thickness
on the sculpted skin
of her impending sex.

To feel with these hands
the swollen mirage
of breasts and hips,
moisture of volcanoes
in the most sensual light
of her restless agony.

To know myself like the god
of an erect power,
relentlessly lying
in her firm fragrance
of garden and half-shadow.

Here is my kingdom,
my decision, my temple,
so in the vehemence
of that insatiable knot,
I may advance and subdue her
till slowly turning her
into my lustful slave.

She

She washes my face stained with hate,
sewing its scars with joyous sutures,
repairs pain, balancing it
with smooth resonances in her young word.

She shoos off those crows so they'll never return
and I soon forget them like an evil dream.

In her hands grows a greenery of caresses
and then, in the most intimate repose,
in my mouth she puts a wine of distant stars,
unfurling her naked rainbow along my body.

So emerges and grows this comforting sun
in brief daytimes of delight.

Almost a Madrigal

So big, it's so big I could
lock it in the sky of my fist,
here beneath the tightened fingers,
as if it were a stubbornly captive god
in the absurd empire of imagination.

I would attack hate with the power of hate,
squeeze it blindly till gradually turning it
into water or even smoke, a crystalline breath,
barely a far-off fragrance
of what was a memory fading away.

It would be a madrigal to show me
the limit of light that belongs to a victory
longing to perpetuate the value of life.

If I Could Conjure Up Their Names

If I could conjure up their names,
bring them down from crests of awful nests,
make them pleasant, free from the moist
loathing they aim from the centre of their slime,
if their chorus of shadows broke up
in this lifeless night without a truce or calm,
if I still had the verve, the faith to rescue them,
if my dense character could mould
the boldness to break the negation
and mineral hate in which they are still captive,
if I dared to look at them face to face,
hear them calmly, be in their hearts
and check the obscure uncertainty,
the crucial instant when the wound appeared,
the sudden bonfire where scorn sprang up,
then, oh my weightless question,
if I had the essence of luck
and the magnet of the most seductive power,
I would be convinced of firm friendship.

Yet I ask: could I perhaps love them
the same way I hate them?

My Dear Enemy

I've no idea why I suddenly hear him
despite the rancour he always wakes in me.
He's occupied my house, taken revenge on my dreams,
sickened the city with my suits,
chooses the jobs I'd have turned down,
insists on their calling him by my name.
With his self-absorption in vain abstractions,
he helps them humiliate and forget me.
Why must he find pleasure when I embrace
that unstaunchable loneliness
so stubborn and cold, so similar to death,
from which only writing saves?
He perceives, and I hardly realize it,
the wind's sound in the night dew.
As soon as dawn rises, he leaves on my table
useless fragrances he brought me from the sea.
He won't let me forget, only wants me to search,
go down to the distance of my directions
and bring him back branches of words
rooted in all I saw.
But I always fail when I try to get free
from his dogged exhausting presence.
And though I whip myself to throw him out,
he consoles me with my own tears.
Who could believe I became his slave
when I forged my first lines on paper?

Mantis

Locked lock.
Blind burnt eyes
tempt desolation
in the body's ritual.

A white-hot black edge
scratches, fouling the air.
Drowning in its saliva,
I feel coldness in my teeth,
steely ice, I turn,
descend to your dementia.

Snatch my aversion,
tear it out by the roots,
suck down to its bile
to forge in stone
all my dark blood.

The heart doesn't exist.
You tore it out live
to plunge it into your rank
fire, devoured it
in its wasps' nest,
making me fierce
as the raped glacier
breathing and shrouding you
in our stingers'
furious light.

Ocellus aging you
to track you, mantis,
in your usury of shadows
and extermination, by being
your own lover, too.

There must be no heartbeat
far from the wound
of this tight copulation,
but a steady, watchful
rancour growing, hushing
always against myself,
by learning from you
death's vice.

Vengeance Considered as One of the Fine Arts

Homage to Thomas de Quincey

Above all things, be patient, stay calm,
submit to impulses, suppress your complaint.
Vengeance has to be a cold pleasure
served in the beauty of a ritual.

For it, one needs its scenography's
perfect sketch, lights and volumes
you foretell, to know and reveal
right to the tiniest detail that may help your task.

Don't forget the influence of that powerful,
clear inspiration. It will lend form, colour,
pleasing harmony to that peerless work of art.

Your canvas is your enemy, his happiness or health.
You should look first carefully
at the complete landscape of his life,
the moral texture, its secrets and vices.

Once you examine the delicate densities
of any sensation or sentiment,
better will be your stroke, finer, more accurate.

Look for the place and time you need.
Accept, therefore, my insistence,
stay calm, be patient, exemplary in your style
to see it rounded off with the supreme glow.

from

Wellspring of Presences

Manantial de las presencias

(1994)

Youth

The wind pleads for peace, writes its armistice
in the wheat fields' looming high tide.
Their whispering moves away in memory . . .
I find you, youth, in that way
of laughing, in the star-studded anguish
you one day sketched in my pupils,
when I invoked a woman's body
to cross with her the borders of fire.
Lines on the horizon. Sea and its surf,
white wavings of beauty
amidst sun and saliva mingled on the sand.
Warm, quivering mirages come back to me.
I recognize you, instants, in the intense harmony
drifting down from fleeting stars.
How can I not love that figure I one day was,
so flowing and lavish, cheerful and adventurous?
Luminous mistakes or late discoveries?
No matter now. Life forgives us
for the simple reason of having burned.

Father

Father, how could I go with you
when your eyes and mine will be
strict eyelids of silence?

And if we turn into separate grasses
in remote countries or silent seas?
How should we know our voices on the wind?

What fragrances, what saps and signals
could I release so butterflies
or bees would carry you my words?

I want to feel your hand in mine,
as when I was a child, beyond the mist
and that dark trance of which we know nothing.

Listen to my unease, its unbearable helplessness.
To know with your absence the house won't be
the earthen bowl welcoming and redeeming me,
nor your forehead the treetop that protects me,
nor your steps the turning of earth
in my brooding heart.

Father, you should have been all my time,
the time elapsing and aging me,
merging in my hours till the end
to turn with you into the same ash.

Even more than time itself,
for example, this unexplainable love,
this dogged nostalgia never leaving,
this steady sheer maelstrom
linking me to life with your name.

Mother

Mother, while I think you're asleep beneath the willow,
you've gone back to your fulsome, blonde youth.
The years went by for us almost without our knowing
in my locked zeal of keeping up the search for words
and dreaming the joy of their insinuations.
Though at times you don't understand my solitary life
from hearing this music of shuddering or shadow,
I know nothing exists to separate us.
Perhaps you're sorry for my dogged silence,
perhaps mortified by the persistent emptiness
of the wait, the prolonged absence
of that far-off son who took with him
the surety of his own hell.
How much life I'd give to get you back,
free from this demand weighing me down
to exhaustion. But I stubbornly tell myself:
she's there, in the beat of my heart,
dreaming me, lighting each lovely memory.

This Sunbeam

You were born in a mystery's leafy half-light,
a warm ray of sun beside the stream,
in the midst of a crystalline siesta
with summer's purest name.

Blue, voluptuous was your shadow,
clean clarity made you quiver.
You radiated an enraptured dance
with forest murmurs and poppies' passion.

I heard a wellspring's gushing.
Then I perceived your gold abundance
sparkling in my fingers like an invincible wave
carrying in its space the wings of wonder.

You burned with the grove's light throbbing,
sketching in air a frenzy of birds,
swaying in the music of a swing of branches.
You were the king of day in your instant of light,
the sharp horizon of a poem.

The Presence of Music

I *Day*

People say a delirium revives the rain
that couldn't fall, makes the leaves quiver,
whispers, syllabifies in the saddest branches
of any longing. Then, only then,
with all anxiety I invoke the fraternal friend –
that mischievous elf of a very lonely childhood –
to find his voice, so in his light he'll carry me
lighting up lanes, leaping over puddles.
He makes the forest stand and wakes the linnet,
sketching the loveliest ribbon in the river,
and banishes tears to their garden of quartz.
With the gust of the wave calling in my ear,
with the moist odour of fragrant earth
and the image of the swan flowing in the morning,
so, with the pulsing of a rebellious heart
in the winging gallop of the wind's horse,
I listen and sense you inexhaustible, Mozart.
I know you hurl and envelop a measureless age,
with the exact sound of your sudden notes
falling and lingering in the clear silences
of memory and sorrow, to rescue it there,
to staunch its wound, to lift it up amidst the fire
of this plentiful quarry that is now transparence,
the breeze of childhood always waiting.

At this hour the iris of the stars lights up.
Their radiant corollas tremble, dripping sky,
and the colours dream of its hidden ringing.
A clock without hands tells the century's peace
as if it heralded a simple miracle.
And suddenly it's everything, it even hushes the air,
forgets memory and the sounds surge.
Sun initiating fire, fire flaring up
with the fervour a boy engrossed in an enigma.
And I rise, spurred on by the soul of space
with its dark deluge of cosmic brotherhood.
The pulsating house living in my body
gently sways, dissolving in cadences,
and everything turns into music, yours,
Mozart, your unquenchable, winging melody,
and you create morning in the world's night
and next to you I remain listening to the light,
listening to the stars, in the enduring core
of this happiness so free it drowns the heart.

Poetry, the Poem

Why does poetry strip us naked, blooming
in the surprise of an absurd instant
we didn't understand before? She dresses the doll
with any paradox. Harlequin, Snow White
or the cunning cat leaping seven leagues?

A poem is a trick teaching a truth,
or perhaps more than a game to elude death,
a skilful magician having no idea
if, in his top hat, there's room for a sylph, an elephant,
Hamlet's certainty or Ophelia's doubt.

Harsh is the loneliness it dreams and writes of.
In the end what it looks for is a bit of love,
though at bottom it intuits that its task
is only for a limbo of amused idlers.

A poem is a gift, a prize or a miracle
that is good for all and for nothing.
It condemns its writer, saves the listener.
Its effectiveness is needed for it aims at the air
and its shot lights up
even the wandering fervour of our hearts.

The Garden of Words

On going through that pass,
he found himself facing an abstract garden
blurring in his pupils.
There dwelled, in their age without dates,
morbid lanterns of words
in noon's high youth.

Engrossed, he sat down with them
to solve the mists of their meanings.
No one understood how he could reach
even that secret place. He stubbornly
remained next to their shadows, barely perceived
suspicious looks and a haughty scorn.

They were part of inaudible wakes,
stripped bare of the masks of signs
by which he knew them. They flowed shining
from a lovely nameless simplicity,
free of all human bondage
as they were the memory of wisdom.

He wanted to be one of them: sea, joy, aroma.
But, tied to his body, he couldn't reach them.
The years slowly went on wiping him out
without his ever managing to grasp their enigmas,
without knowing he had turned
into the exact word of dreams.

Shadowy Helmets

Breathe easy and heed the signs.
Above the river, night thickens with stars
in a confusion of thunder and cloudscapes.
With horses of mist and sheets of nickel,
with shadowy helmets, they spring from the waters.
It's the dead's inaudible hour.
Watch them fill the horizon,
decked in seaweed erased by the mud,
with blind eyes and the severest grimace.
They march ahead disorderly and cross
the drawbridges of your mind.
Too late to turn them back, to excuse yourself.
They hunt for the wandering tower of dreams
to take up with you and share
the indecisive's abysmal limit.
Indivisible as loneliness and art,
like the dream of soul and lust,
they are your inner phantoms,
frivolity's harsh enemies.
Though you won't admit it, they're more yours
than your ancestral nostalgia or rebellion,
perhaps your defencelessness facing the delirium
of being every day the unnamed guest
of yourself, or that other figure, also you,
but without the sorrow of having deserted you.
Listen to them: all the actions
of your life, the fervour and remorse
time interred. Now they call you.
Lift your glass, toast, celebrate them!
May they not turn to stone, but sing blazing
and go with you faithfully to forgetting!

Lines of Mystery

A profile. A rough profile returning his face.
A scribble sketching fatigue.
A tattoo watching you from its own well.
What dialogue, what sad inhuman babble
spreads out between the emptiness of paper
and your blind empty heart?

The drawing delays its walk,
deepening, subduing its trace.
Unforeseen shadows of pain,
a sign of light, emerging woodlands.
Patiently you choke the mutiny of doubts.

Harsh lines scratch his contour.
Through black holes now looms
the vision you project. A curve insinuating
a scornful, compassionate lip.
Hair stealing from the crow its sinister reflection.

The faith of the creator doggedly illuminates
the slight resemblance to that figure he invents.
Strokes that withdraw in the end, shading off.
A path travelling itself and in itself foreseeing
the ember of life, a certain uncertain miracle.

You light a cigarette, draw near,
go down to the depth of his genes
to install the dizziness of a breath.
The smoke of dreams invades, penetrates him.
'Look at me straight!' you say. 'Get up!
Live now without me the freedom of your fate!'

Sleepless Ceremony

Towering as an irreversible fate,
a flaking wall surrounds me,
the only reference, unvarying days
and nights. I see clouds float by
so unresolved and alien,
the gusty suns weave a chiaroscuro,
the phantasmagoric net swinging
like an endless ceiling of oceans.
I have only this wall, the wall's throbbing.
The years taught my eyes
to see on stones the feverish histories
told by moisture, civilizations slowly
succeeding each other, furiously self-devouring,
exiles and struggles, burial mounds of fire,
a world of roots, ships, blazes, copulations,
beneath the instant's varied stars.
At the end of a long forgetting,
the senses expectantly warn me.
The moon gleams a bed of mercury,
raises its tantalizing thirst, the greediest delirium.
I hear how the murmuring wall calls me.
Its link with time blinds and unifies.
Tribes of green veins whose sap
comes from the dead dissolved by clay
pour their troubled marrow into the naked
interstices of my body to make it fuller's earth.
A sleepless ceremony of seeding shadow
hurls its blackened existence,
its inconsolable breath of frenzied jungle:
thick migrations of insects and flying things
now pierce my eyes, furrowing my arteries,

mixing with them in tumults, in harsh,
zigzagging gusts, violent frights,
like a hollow of blood sucking its blood
till locking it up in this dark wall
suddenly looming not to leave us behind.

from

Oasis of a Cosmos

Oasis de un cosmos

(1994)

Summer Stars

Cleave, fiery vessels, through winds of torment.
Rise to the height of desire
with a furious surf's green thrust.
Who showers you with bonfires in your budding
enigma? Who commands that inviolate essence
in a flight of abysses? What do you put in my eyes
so I always dream you? Flowers of inebriation,
keep me company with your fertile spell.

Be the light of this song securing your name,
its inspiration and jubilance, the time of my force
in your eternity's flame-eating expanse.
What unease of metaphors in eloquent breeze,
what a silent explosion beneath supreme glass.
From what sleeping mirrors are you the splinters?
Tell me how much light from that light
have you stubbornly guarded.
In what huge combs do you keep God's honey?

You are fright and ember in polished beauty,
surprised manna, gold dust
overflowing, raining from the blue precipice,
blinking magma of invisible volcanoes,
neighbourhood of night coming down with vertigo,
clarity reaching us from luminous ancestries,
eyes of tenderness and flood
from which shines the heaven we cannot see.

Dazzling heralds of all boundaries,
waves of lapis lazuli, sap from the new dawn,
you sculpt the metope of the soul,
scattering smiles with myriads of echoes.

Yes, I'm he who's born when he gazes at you
growing in infinite rainbow prisms.
Only this way do I turn into the ocean
that crosses starry distances,
stripping the shadows bare in whiteness,
wearing in pupils my childhood victories.

Enthralling summer stars,
you come in the branches of sleeping birch
with a dream of light and woodland fragrances
in the skewed wind of fable.
Spilling spring, fullness of free waters,
stampeding string of sorrels, alabaster in lightning bolts.
You are my trip in the sleeping valley's
calm, invoking life
with the passion of the sea hurling to shore
trembling mirages rising in the foam.

Summer stars with youthful voices
and a clear whisper of sirens,
you paint with your snow the lunar wakes
and the dew of clover in its welcoming way.
You are grander than the world and in a drop of water
merge with the sun that wakes me.
You look at me suddenly from wine,
turning the perfumed rainbow of the south.

Life gives you the colour of instants
and in my glass you dance with dazzled sails,
with the wise lust of an unburning fire
and heaven's magic in the blood.
I rise up to your zenith and am a tree
and, in my Olympus of branches, I receive you.
The world, the whole universe is yours
as you increase its liberty in your light.

I Only Know Your Strangeness

I still drink on the star of silence,
still breathe and write. Watch my hand flow
beneath this aura of stars with everlasting bonfires
lighting crystals and distances.

Who are you, inspiration? I only know your strangeness.
You come to drown me in your dark smile,
for you inhabit the night of a stanza
whose verb begins in a shudder.

For me the rapture of this verse is enough,
hunting for me a truce to postpone death.

To write is an art bringing distances near,
still the most distant in memory,
the cricket's song lifting the planet's psalm;
love, too, the fingers caressing
a woman's startled breast
or a space waiting to split into halves
from which time exudes its essential truth.

To write is to gaze into deepness,
to lend colour and form to bodies in refulgence,
to exchange the void's blackest holes
for a blue cosmos with golden oranges,
to feel the universe in a child's eyes,
the unfading light: revelation.

You, my hand, lean on its dense lightning,
rise again with the swift wing of the unweary.
Look, look with all your powers,
set upright the tree offering you its shade

and wake the torrent and its flight
to the heartbeat of shared soul,
there above, here nearby, in its enamel garden,
where the word, in sparkling, crosses:
I touch, breathe it, and listen to the world.

The Firmament Sails

Like a calm transparent sailboat
vibrating between its trembling lamps,
late summer's firmament sails,
heralding the features of autumn.
Its horizon is a circle of flight and victory.
The futile rots away, the impossible tempts me,
the longed for settles in with its sheen.

Amidst the most visible and invisible,
the look slowly lifts
towards a garden of fire and faraway.
Hives of planets beyond nocturnal suns
and the constellations we cannot see.
Their windows in flames seem to console us
for it's the universe looking at us through them.

Silence anoints us with its clement clarity,
the austere parade dazzles us,
the huge ship with its bright candelabras floats by.
Splendours, spilling, transfix us,
penetrating the soul with a murmur of pines,
the light releases the reins and starts to dream.

In the embers' night anxiety,
certainty reaches the heart anew.
The eyes, seduced, become a world.
In the sure peace of branches
abysses of fragrance grow thick.
The moon wheels, indigoing dragonflies.
In the air's celestial music
a sacred impulse, a radiance
are revealed by words that mirror night
in fragile crystals of dew.

There's a Point of Light Pondering Us

In the deepest dip of any road,
next to the abysmal edge of feeling
or in the intimate wreck of bitter news,
there's a point of light pondering us
with the humble calm of knowing
we're never alone. That light watching over us
with a bonfire's loving fervour
that pulses in you and me, in all our dreams,
retains the intensity of fear that knows itself
condemned to go out in its short-lived life.
Yet that core of love embracing us
beyond death and the metamorphoses
experienced by the invulnerable soul,
that point trembling in our hearts,
is the solar centre of the universe.

The Forest of Stars

Stars trembling in my enigmas,
pulsing of branches and fire's polish,
steady eyes of tigers lurking for me,
hecatomb of arrows in flight
where the hour lights its black of lightnings.

You are the country of my nights,
the only earth of my dark blood.
You waver facing the wind like fountains
with their prisms of signs growing among shadows
in a still jungle towards incandescence.

What a privilege to be in heaven's canvas,
what a plenitude of sparks, what blue gifts.
Your embrace is brightness in suspense,
an invading delight of inventions,
a torrent of victorious night
beyond the trampled limits.

In night splendour, space is ecstasy,
a wellspring of presences dissolving in the light.
It reaches me like a powerful wave
flowing and spreading amidst all existing.

Crowned confines, reefs of suns,
I offer you my being, whole now,
with burning energy unfolding
in a winged instant of oneness.

In the Beech Forest

From stray paths springing up in space
to the thick foliage of beech,
exhausted, a stream of sun slips down.
Beneath the sunset the grove sways,
alerting murmurs in half-light.
The wind whistles captive as a conch
in which sea is heard, heaven's high sea.

Something's unexpected in the landscape,
an impulse breaking its stillness,
a dark fright, a trembling, a force.
The roots grind, the masts wave
beneath a harsh surf suddenly enraged.

I lift my gaze to huge treetops
and feel there's a green firmament
where the branches blend together
like the clashing of violent swords.
Steeds collide, lightning bolts explode
in their escaping constellations.

The storm increases, lashes the mirrors,
runs, floods over the trunks
with the vision of a cosmos bled
by warriors of luckless dynasties
that never manage to halt their struggle.

There, in some place of memory,
they go on battling beneath the rain,
condemned to be their own death,
without their even being able to discover
the pity that moves the heart of man.

The Hour of Clover

There, in the night's whirlwind,
in the palate of an invisible mouth,
like galleons gone adrift
with their drunken lamps in the wind,
off course, adrift for unknown millennia,
like words fixed in oblivion,
stars beam with insomnia.

I feel summer's growing throb
in the carnal fragrance of flowers.
Salamander eyes bustle in the cracks
beneath the willows' motionless abulia.
Stillness and its roulette of crouching moons.

A handful of clover is the world's luck.
Its memories are peopled with dew,
with fiery horses from the vicious gale.
Look, look here at the instant and its magic,
the instant enveloping perplexed night.

The mountain passes light up in the breeze
as though still searching for the stealthy trees
that fled from their stony cliff of shadows.
The invisible appears in the air and disturbing
presences of no wind reappear,
the flock and chirpings of accent and tilde.
Here the furious exclamation
sets the landscape on its knees.

Nightingales come with fiery undertows
and an owl ponders the enigma's text.
Only jasmine is frightened, turning pale with snow.

The cones of pines, rocked by the air,
wheel like the stars tilling their aroma
in a leafy sky of woodlands.

I inhale, open my eyes to the slow vision
of this vegetal light. I hear its whispering
facing epigrams sketched by mist
and dark matter's grave murmurings.

Where the wind hides before the stampede,
and the riot of leaves raises its dance,
the incarnation of metaphors flows,
unfolding their genesis powers.
I live here, and in you, loyal nature.
Death doesn't know us yet.

Father Universe

This afternoon, so slow, effusive and mine,
this afternoon of peace that doesn't capsize,
throbs in its perspective of horizons
with all of a firmament starting to constellate,
to light up red distances adrift.

This afternoon, absolute in its strangeness,
overwhelms, reduces down to whatever limit
the unfinished point I still am.
I ask myself what there'll be beyond silence.
Shall I keep some memory of life?

Father Universe, leave me the fervour
I once felt on this earth,
only to celebrate you with my awkward,
inconstant, scant human love.

The Abandoned Star

From the firmament's fertile breeze,
humiliated, a moan descends,
the lonely trembling of a star.

Perhaps, because of the beauty of its light
or the untameable pride of knowing its fate,
petrous powers dispatched it
to the end of its cycle in the galaxy.

From what hunch of mine comes its sobbing?

What incomprehensible, cloudy distance
rises like surf from my heart,
driving me towards a depth I divine?

In its wandering rotation I feel the firmness of weeping
and I'm reached and moved by an echo in space.

Ellipse of Another Rose

When a rose blossoms, a feeling swirls
of a world beginning. There's something
dazzling in its splendour of shared abyss,
reflecting an oasis of silence,
a constellation of virgin springs
in whose waters buds light kindling dawn.

She is her own dream preceding her image,
a gift of intimacy, the soul of memory,
the vision of an essence beaming the firmament
from leafy petals of breeze.

Earth's fire rings her crown
so none will forget her starry lineage
and she emerges from herself like a ghost,
a goddess who's dared to live with us
the ephemeral dream of days
to give us the eternal's sudden nostalgia.

Legend of a River

And we shall wake up fascinated,
lying on the grass of a darkening star.
Happy to offer ourselves, right to the end we'll
let the unknown teach and take us
towards the intensity that makes the bonfire flare.
We'll be the mirror in which desire sings.

May white-hot night bind us in her embrace,
her headiness of absolute boundaries.
And so, the instant we longed for fulfilled,
we'll go unhurriedly into our waters
and make ourselves always the same river.

The Bird Apprentice

When dusk was dyed with mists,
he climbed the bell tower with a fish net
and listened to ocean join the air.
He collected flights, multicoloured wings,
trillings, melancholies of forest and gold,
sunset's lost birds.
He turned his home into a huge nest
where the unusual flocks that tore
the wind grew old and flew.
He patiently tended them till he grew invisible,
as if before their eyes he were only a tree,
a part of time or breeze.

He spied their beginnings, the awkward movement,
the way of hunching up in a limbo of feathers,
the first position of flanks planned
for the learning of flights.
He registered it all in his memory,
their ritual and habits, the hours of their song,
the tiniest imperceptible gesture:
picking with beak in down,
the semiconfidentiality, the brusque wooing,
the nails outstretched as if pondering,
calculating the space foreseen
in the toes' retractile tautness.

After divining the most secret laws
of the flock's restless tribe,
he set out to meet his yearning.
He opened the large full windows wide
and in jubilant rivers, in winged torrents,

in a spiral of sudden shadows,
the birds flew off towards the sky.

Then he remembered his stubborn apprenticeship,
counted the winds, distances,
moistures and his slow shuddering,
calculating his weight's volume in air.
And he prepared the difficult, challenging course.
He leapt firmly, winning the void,
wildly opened his arms,
knowing his home would always be
infinite, dazzling space.

Baclava

From an ecstatic orient of zithers and silks,
on magic carpets of puff pastry
down comes memory's sweetest word.
In my ears revolves its celestial sound
of bewitching syrup, of cinnamon
breathing in air enraptured honey.

Dripping, it turns into a dance of gold,
a dune's fascination, a savouring
that drugs with its lightning name:

baclava! Suddenly the mouth becomes a spring,
a sonorous ship, a canticle, haunting arpeggios
transporting me over sparkling rivers,
and the stars soar like blissful bees
through the seven senses of a lustful universe.

Cosmogony

Astounded, he felt the ceiling of nothingness
erasing the existence of meaning and time.
Whose was that persistent hand?

It was the same hand from the beginning,
the one that separated light from doubts and chaos.
Over space it unfurled its flight,
reordering planets and solitudes.

He dreamed a disturbing theory,
maybe the most fertile one, without granting a place
to the truth of verse. Could he be a creator,
a visionary plotting his parable?

Leave him in peace. Allow him
the useless fantasy of an instant.
Let him fix the world, let's see if he then keeps quiet.

The Fire's Constellation

A distant language from the embers wheels
in the air of the fire. That red spiral whose dance
dreams me has a sacred breath,
a crystalline mystery I intuit alone
in the instant's waking constellations.

At the same time the sparks go out,
in the flames I glimpse the heartbeat of the stars,
hear the voice, make out some words
I futilely try to interpret.

I only reveal a plea, its evidence,
a tangible tenderness flowing in night dew
as if it would send me in its longing
a forgotten memory, my cosmic otherness.

Nocturnal Plea

In night's lofty wakefulness,
I invoke stellar powers
with a cry coming from the void.
I respond to the call of what's strange,
trembling, oceanic forces
create the unique image, springing
from it as if the sea rose up in the air
and were wholly just one wave
greater than life in its galaxies.
Night is the vast ambience appealing
to the silent birth of verses.
It's not enough to be the peak of an instant,
the longed-for, undestroying plenitude.
The secret is speech that flares
and links us in the night, writes us
the words we are and shall be.

Lonely Affliction

Only death hatches her heartbeat in my wound,
uncertain frugality, the cold's slow heat.
She digs in her wet mine of shadow and chrysanthemums
and in the willows I listen to the sentencing voice.
Night invisibly approaches, overwhelms
the silence, feeling my prison in the dark,
this city without a name where heavenly bodies
with maws of millennia devour distances
I'll never have to see, and the words fly off
as if they couldn't measure the void,
slight cracks that pretend what's always hidden
in my lonely affliction. Tired out, I resist
being this ash barely inflamed
by the sun of an instant, though soon the gloom
will come, splitting blue distances,
carrying a mote of dust up to the stars.

Soul of the Universe

I know this night's gentle air
lights an anguish, a distance
searching for the answer to this love for the cosmos.
Each star's a point of giddy light
flowing in the current running through my veins
as if it were the soul of the whole universe
that breathed unanimously in my blood.

You are a mirror, a pulse, an unceasing fate
drawing me to its star-filled centre,
the most fragrant glass from which I drink
my strict loneliness with the absolute.
How can I rise till I reach your fullness,
with what resonant courage in the word
so you open your arms and receive me?

Now I see myself naked and proffered,
free from the ambition of being my own challenge,
with the thirst for fusing into your cosmic music,
like one simple note of the hymn rising
through the timeless breezes of your name.

from

Embers of Nadir

Ascuas del nadir

(1995)

1   Night

Everlasting surf. The sea hurling diamonds
against the rocks. With its boyish boldness
it thrusts from on high sudden groves,
lights, gabbling of gulls,
harsh green panthers against the untouched sand.

The sea unfolds the iris of the blue,
shaking its sieve through which star-strewn
night and its red fires filter.
Calmly it deciphers signs of gold,
barely a moment shines amidst the pebbles
with its dazzling free smile
borne on the whispering of winds.

And in the darkness buzz faint starry castanets,
the phrasing of an invisible oracle
on danger's supreme summit.
In all its radii glitters the blazing symmetry,
the torrent of waves a turn of orators,
cries and controversies, deaf quarrels
of spume and stone in their broken swings.

The mistral's bitterness and violence
in the never-ending struggle
breaking, scattering crystal seams.
From unconquered maelstroms it hurls
its legends, lively images,
ancient exorcisms, banished histories
of civilizations and sombre seasons.

What impatient, what strange useless pomp,
the tones of so many pyrotechnics,

and how many sculptures of shattered glass
in the unforeseen second of lightning,
smashing the glory of its cruel beauty
like fugacity's fearless symbol.

Sleepwalking sea, obsessed, you twist, howl
in your constant milky seething,
a furor, greedy bronze prisoner,
invested in your abrupt black lacquer.
From thick towers your throbbing quivers
through electric medusas and in sailboats lying to,
hiding the unfathomable's dread.

Spouting sea, thunderous sea, you bind yourself
demented to a secret alliance of misfortunes.
You leap over balustrades, topple snowy temples
and columns, corrode the statues
of any human god and nothing withstands
your stubborn unrelenting whim
or your resplendent display.

And you sink and strip yourself,
luxurious vagabond, self-devouring nadir,
with the blindest rancour faced with your force,
and you unfold phosphoric sails
in a sudden trip against lunar grottos.

Something remains floating amidst the breeze,
an agile murmur of blue-black vine leaves
in the cosmic placenta's peace.
Suddenly I notice the splashing
of two oars crossing the bay
beneath the rain's minute power.

When you sleep, only a bluebottle
beside your ear manages to wake you
from nightmares and regrets.
To swell once more arteries and tendons,
that risk, that avalanche of your ample anatomy
forgetting its harm's fate.

From where this bellowing growing from the waters?
What perverse condemnation, what mystery
summons me from its occult outcry?
What dark pages, what untranslatable book
perpetually stirs the feeling of the waves?

One could say you drown the noisy pack of fire,
that the fear of your own delirium
unfolds its prayer at your feet.
You turn the moving echo, organ of the din,
vortex, riot, seaweed's bellows
blowing from sunken labyrinths
where invisible divers labour
to tune up celestial machinery,
undulating gears of miracle.

Protector of Atlantis submerged in your centuries,
you rush swiftly from the distance,
irreconcilable, strange, damned in your desert,
with the misty tear ranging the planet.

You spring up like age in quicksilver
remembering the date of death.
You lay down sentences, diffuse illusions,
indefinitely defendable.
There's a world beneath the waves,
a sombre silence of tacit bells

that have forgotten their monotonous tolling
amidst the tremulous throbbing of the abyss.

Oceanic disorder. The waters beget
with that tumultuous identity.
Surfs of different stock
united, divided again by your torment.
Bereft of strength, you weigh down defenceless
to lend movement to spaces.
Green blood grows budding from your slime.
And you come and go, return and curse,
turn entreating and, forgotten, disappear
in short and idle intervals.

A battle front of drums advances and forms up;
your troops assault the ochre reefs,
waterfalls rise with boilers seething,
high horses grow from which trees emerge,
trees slowly fading into the clouds,
storm clouds laughing their light rain
on jewels and clovers of surprised north wind.

At times I glimpse you caged in your waves,
captive amid the dreams of your aquarium,
in the faces of secret instants,
in the fears of some memories of the future,
when our past is that insufficient alms
to buy the hour advancing towards us.

Hear it in its magnetic stampede,
screeching horseshoes of centaurs
vibrate against metal sheets
and the thunder bellows, beats the distances
with its white-hot stony hammer

waking sparks and heartbeats
throughout all the salt's horizon.

A crevice opens. There comes the herd
of that seething gold boundary
and blindly they thrust their foreheads
against the sand banks' golden wall.
The glaucous light floods its freest flash
with a metaphor's oblique passion
longing to keep well within its sphere
the thirst, the fit, the frenzied struggle,
grievous and futile, of human existence.

Perplexingly hoarse, that neighing revives,
a chained god's gloomy lament.
A black sun crosses, like a dagger in shadow,
nocturnal horizons, shrouds
helmets, breastplates, plumes, beheaded steeds
in the umbrous forests of the depths.

Look at its irreducible undertow.
See how its angriest germ grows,
stripping the stones of the beach.
Go off quickly, flee its lure.
Don't you see it wraps us in its hypnotic sobbing?

But its grandeur's not that proud trance
in cruel, desolate prairies so convulsed.
Its danger's fertile dimension
is the slow-motion descent to the unknown.
All light goes out, every cry in the air
gradually fades into a stupor.

And gradually farther, blinding its mirage,
the shining roofing of that surface

delicately gripped by the moon.
Unredeemed fall towards a core of shadows,
towards blackness without breath, spaceless fall,
fainting indefensible suction,
unusual descent beneath the weight
of all the powers of the waters.

Through unknown turbulences
and different climates of the cold,
you descend, keep falling with sleepwalking lucidity.
You slip on slopes repulsive to touch,
barely see, don't smell, surprised
by phosphoric presences, abject flappings,
vibrating foreshortenings, fog and its profiles,
maws like caves with myriads of eyes.
Stray cables tie sunken ships,
rags of sails like sorrowful flags
of wars and defeats, sticky messengers
with broken shrouds scorned by death.

You fall beneath a sudden abyss,
irresistible thrust toward a hidden fault.
Its undertow sleeplessly drags you
with a crouching hate's obsession.
You roam among assaulting sharks,
vaults narrowing in a lethal sway.
From their half-open teeth sprout
slow bubbles like quicksilvers
and in each one images of silent oblivion,
images of ghosts reflecting
your eyelids glassy with agony.

Fish-scale maelstroms turn in the current,
confronting your cornered body
with the thick tautness of breath.

A grasping force in its funnel swiftly
sinks you hallucinating towards depth and dark.

You don't slip but fall, fall continually,
dragged, driven, not knowing through which vertigos,
among ropes and masts. Swarthy ashen polyps
hunt you with violent tentacles,
you flee, go on fleeing indefinitely,
not knowing to what core, to what refuge,
hopelessly alone, alone and alone.
A chorus of bubbles accompanies you;
perhaps it's the only answer
to what was your life, your end.

Like a bulk without bearings, you go down
with eyes open and hands astray.
You keep falling confused, always going
into the sea that's going through your marrow,
as if it would decide another abyss in your blood,
opening an unending descent in memory
towards an anonymous cosmos without ages or limits,
endlessly condemned to go on
hurled into the dark of your dream.

Sea, my inmost sea, I wake on the leafy shore
from the fables you intone for me.
Here with visions breathing and waving,
I foresee your deepest depths' murky crystals
in the retina's radiant flames.
Don't I belong, perhaps, to that enigma
man believed hell's primordial home?

I ask you for the word that's reborn
and remains faithful in my writing,
the unfainting anguish, your forms' throbbing,

the clear fervour so natural to your force,
your thrill of silences, your vibration and rhythm.

I am lit up by a fire in the water,
its impure vortex flashes till it blinds,
it lends me the vehemence of a dark disquiet,
defended only by your waves.

The dogged unruly echo extends
to the rocky cold of constellations
beneath a halo's ring of kettledrums.
Time's intensity stands enraptured,
captive in the night's drowned ivy.

Huge is the sea's heart. Feel it.
It's there in its prison of vertigos and water
and in our ear sings: 'Life's born from me.
In me earth's psalms spring up.

'I'm that sailing ship ploughing the kindled
orchards of dream. I explore underwater
cities, calm typhoons,
I blind their hellish Cyclopes' eyes,
I flatten their vengeful grape harvests
in the blackest chasms of the abyss.

'At times I'm a stubborn hummingbird
sucking in sapphires of the night,
profusely alive in joy,
the quickest herald of unceasing dawn.
I am the figurehead of sparks
waking in the doors of dew,
unfolding its canvas to the morning.

'Today I want you at my side. Wake up.
You have to be watchful with dreams open,
hearing my gardens of drunken lechery.
Come with me to the waters' kingdom,
there where eyes were never witnesses,
in the waves you'll feel your impulse of fish
beneath my inescapable freedom.

'What a deep flight through coral valleys.
The water's always a lithe breeze caressing
your body. It binds it delicately
with the liveliest crystal suit
to give you a constancy of pleasure.

'My body's unending delight,
a fascinating game, an always fresh bed,
a centre or swirl of hollows and embraces
with an odour of epics and fullness of roses,
a swing of sighs and reflections,
a magic floating amidst marine wings
raised on a fire that doesn't burn.

'How explain, imagine or be
the possible out of all the impossible
in my successive metamorphoses?
Come with your awkward steps
from arid regions of desolate suns.
I'll erase the unstaunched wound,
that tense longing for all you lack,
with the same glow of surprise
as the water that springs from thirst.

'I am the light of a countless beam
piercing the shade of colours
in the morning's solar uproar.

Know this home, feel welcome,
but respect the breath, the wavy murmur
of each being throbbing and defending itself
in the communal gift it suggests,
for life's the soul's insurrection,
an urge freeing itself from its own spirit
to inhabit its welcoming kingdom.'

Don't be silent, sea, go on in ringing sorcery
with your astonished white pursuit,
go on in your irrepressible night
where we are the fertile harmony of a time
perhaps unrepeatable in my existence.

Oh, magic subversive power,
in calm you seem a reclining woman,
the skin startled at any touch
with its fragrance of female and black wine,
bright gem encrusted in the country of grass,
you, imagination of adventure,
sun and night follow you, revere your passing.
You are blue laughter lighting the universe.

High votive flame of smoking manes,
you vomit and gather in sad coves
the answers and slimes of shadows,
demented litanies of evil's negligence,
a disturbing combat of music and half-lights,
so umbilically prisoner
in its superior cosmogony,
in which it's impossible to understand your infinite
though we intuit the sacred breath
as essence of a numen denying us when we're created.

In this living forest that's you and my body,
in the perfect instant of this gust
to which I unite your dream in these syllables,
you are hopelessly the thirst sustaining me,
the wellspring of all that's born,
the seed of genesis and its fertile lament,
the word trembling at our asking.
You never tire, never does one forget your impatience
of waiting for the clouds, the air's uneasiness,
the flexible sailboat almost defenceless on your course,
with sails wet and bow towards the south.

You, the breath and soul of beings
surrounding the light of the invisible,
living and protective eternity,
desire's insatiable obsession,
and you go on and advance your horsemen
on the white-hot rumps of pride,
with suits of armour for emphasis and violet glows
to vanquish, at last, the morning.

And a sobbing of sirens emerges from the depths.
Look how their crystal faces glow,
the nostalgia of quartz, jade and its density,
amber and its sky of illusory promises,
beneath the waters' unfading vault,
in this, their voices', raised instant
against the stony sphinx of the world's silence.

from

A Whisper of Agony

Rumor de la agonía

(1996)

Facing the Fire-Light

In my house, I keep a book whose pages speak.
They have no lines, illustrations or verses.
It's a conch shell where I listen to the sea
of pain and life's whisper.
Hearing it, I recover the fright
of future time, its shadow's dagger
cutting candlewicks, setting up dates
of those I know and those I don't.
I have no need to explore it, but it reappears,
dazzling my nights with its music,
losing me in a constant labyrinth.
Since it has named me as confidant,
I feel a fresh compassion for everything existing.
Its wisdom has given me lessons of ignorance
and an ironic smile that dupes misfortune.

Misfortune

With harsh, choking patience,
I go on in vain to survive,
hugging my heartbeat, my possible breath.
The words fled with their meanings,
weightless, without predictions or promises,
without the faith and love that listens to them.

They flew off as if they were brazen dragonflies
escaping to the other side of oblivion.
I don't know what I've no idea of, all's so confused
I pay no mind and grow silent. I keep touching whitewash,
high captive walls, where a lonely instant
suddenly accosts me, like old age
sinking its wreck in my eyes.

On the verge of everything invaded,
I feel a brusque heartbeat, a rain of rubble
falling with the unruly vexing
a chill of misfortune uses to bind me.

This enemy substance searches, tracks,
surrounds, grows inside.
Springs from cruelty's steady shadow,
lifts its old flame of unhappiness
with an unflagging insomnia, with its fury and rancour,
facing the mirror's suicidal pupils.

Could this uninhabited peace,
this restless, incurable breathing,
be the abandoned depth of anguish?
Who could deny or contradict it?

I keep nothing in my hands, nothing of what I had,
but in them I possess the fainting weight
of all the absences and body of emptiness,
that cold, thick essence of pain.

Unremembering

His suits no longer hang from the blind lamps,
nor does madness glitter in the house.
Like a sinking city,
sorrow and loneliness die in the body.
Not even this one, though it continues, is witness,
for time changes it like the boy and his laughter.

When all is lost, even memory itself,
when not even sadness exists, what's left?
Fear, perhaps, destitute fear
facing the greedy air by which we're devoured.

Inkling of dawn. Who warns? An owl
screeches his dread, an anguish with no name.
The hour briefly breaks up.
The light firmly winnows seeds
and I watch without zeal, time or fright
this stray shadow beneath my unremembering.

Facing a Line by Salvatore Quasimodo

'So little time is needed to die by living'
I read in a book. I was dumbfounded, struck
by its certainty's fatal chill.
At what instant did daily death arrive
to live with me once and for all?

Boundary of childhood, savage cut
suddenly separating reality and dream.
Unbelievable surprise in the grief,
when discovering the illusory Eden
is only a stage set, and its beings, masks
hiding old age and bitterness.

Or did it begin afterwards, when the lover
was the most ephemeral flower, and lasting friendship
an accident of mutual convenience?

I am the wandering cemetery
carrying its affections buried in itself.
The rest of life is a rusty noise,
the sadness of hearing my old death.

The Prodigal's Surrender

A bitter awakening probing the intangible.
Insidious prophecy in trails of moon.
A sombre ocean of round flanks thrashes
and gallops in concave empty echoes
of the night dew's habitations.

A man crosses the carnal air of statues,
voices of what's dying torment, harass him,
climbing to the heart of his own misery.
He still doesn't want to leave, grasps at the living
like an ignorant wound beseeching
what sinks in hurt with further fury.

Once more he plunges into the enchantment
life extends: the trap of pleasure,
degradation's obscene splendour.
Sluggish pavements of scorn
make way in the deserted city's fog.

Howl, dog, howl against the dawn.
Insult your breed beneath this ocean air
of damned isle inhabited by ghosts
begging for the dark slavery of gold.

To fall, get up, pound what door of tears?
Everything climaxed in you till you surrendered.
That is your roving guilt, your condemnation.
To be silent facing the leprosy of dreams,
fingering the ash of what could have been.

The Shadowy Alliances

In this ravaged hour when tedium
takes hold of all the murmuring of things,
the cold shadow of wreckage arrives
amidst the endless and confused.

An alien substance without restraint
fatally multiplies in what you loved.
Its clear heartbeat betrays you.
Something undefined. A drowsiness grows huge
as a wave near your shore,
spreading and sweeping towards oblivion
the concern for your essential names.

Weary fever, anguish for everything humiliated.
Your vigil's so hand-tied
you've no idea if death is breathing in your eyes.
Vain sentimentality hankering to corrupt you.
In what stubborn inertia have you fallen?
Nothing or no one now fills your heart,
not even the truce of your song.

Here on this horizon of stars and dunes,
where the sea's soaked with shadowy alliances,
you curse now the names of that impassioned
youth, only to avoid the injury
deified by a hellish stupor.

Love's Agony

Like mysterious locked forces meeting
in the secret depth of an embrace,
emphatically touching each other as though discovering
the rare intimacy that calls them,
convinced and alone, they cling to desire,
that dense confusion of invading each other
with no holds barred or pause, without a breath of caution.
Like hostile, starving animals
spurring each other horribly in the dark,
drinking their smells, mixing their spittle,
rubbing, biting, setting on each other
till the selfsame shedding of blood,
till being the blaze of the other body upraised,
till knocking it down and exhausting it, and broken
and collapsed, transfixed with semen and lust,
like two drunken gods rising once more
from the ashes of their own bonfire
to die and be born afresh in blindness,
they revive, obsessed, over and over,
till they nearly exist no more in the agony,
the corrosive passion of love.

Of Pulp and Wine and Vein

I could never tire of blazing beneath her bonfire.
In her I was thirst and impulse
and the anguish of seeking her eager undulation.
I felt the round nakedness of her breasts,
suns of indolence, tame bolts of lightning.
Her pubis magnetically attracted with earthy depths,
raising the monument of desire.
With her I went down to the white heat,
hearing the coldest greed
bound to the swirl of her fury.

How could I survive the harm of her offering,
her impure tenderness, the moon-struck passion
where each moment was a lascivious sheen
of lashing caresses, of steep thrust,
of jubilant, tense maze
through non-being and being utterly astray?

All was combustion, astonished delight,
sudden still dance and soaring stillness,
sweet fiery pulse, drunken knot of ecstasy,
of pulp and wine and vein of hell
in a heaven fleshed with torment and fragrance.

Never in Your Eyes

Now never again shall I have in your eyes
the sea and its delirium, nor the feeling of your body
scorching me in its bonfire anguish,
nor the October rain blurring streets
as if, by dreaming, the city created me
in the deepest space of your eyes.

Yet the thankful flame
of love, in its strange silence, still unfolds
inconsolable days so that light
slowly extends through the shadows
of another city lost in your mirage.

Beyond this cold where fear welcomes
I read your gestures, decipher your semblance
with the same sorrow belonging to an abandoned world,
without wanting to accept that your eyes gave me,
in lasting enchantment, eternity that dies.

A Tantalizing Fate

Sunk in the wreck of loathing,
sunk down to the oblivion of guilt,
he goes on burying himself. Delirium and maze,
death rattles of life badly told
on the reverse of what was love.

Meanness, silence, accomplice of predators
in the treacherous night dew of harm.
Night riddled with obsessive wings,
insatiable alliances plotting the cliff,
huge drops, countless drops
of calumny raining in his soul,
spoiling the essence of life.

Everything that zeal raised in the air,
erased, unjustly humiliated, darkened.
And he crosses lightning bolts, thirst astray,
imaginary mirrors, banished ghosts,
the dual stage set of existence.

He queries himself constantly, still searching
for the possible ember in which humility
dwells, self-renunciation.
Run aground on his desire, he insists, keeps on
cutting the underbrush of any negation;
and, uplifted, castled in his calm,
he recovers and clutches the reins of challenge.

The heart, a powerful horse,
carved in the pride of what's undefeated, goes on,
doesn't flag and advances, crosses the desert,
swift, dogged, heading for the flowery city.

Enigma in the Sand

How is it possible he came out so?
Perhaps he didn't reach the valuable numbers
demanded by an obsessed ambition?

In his eyes glows the grandeur of day,
the sea's freedom, the triumph of love
in high summer's leisurely morning.

But reality wove its web,
a well-hidden winter trap
in the contemplation of beauty.

The night full of stars has fulfilled
his nostalgia, the badly healed scars
from when he was burned by the absolute.

Maybe, not knowing, he set
the evidence aside, the concrete instinct facing things,
the prearranged place preceding ruin.

Engrossed in his honeycomb, he sucked words
with the bonfire's vehement dance,
impulse, green fire, waves whipping up,
chance and lightning with its steely power.

Suddenly, fatally, the hour arrives
when reverie turns to smoke,
proud horses vanish,
a quiet collapse, enigma in the sand.

The Statue

I slipped carelessly on the slope
and rolled back to the shortcut's beginning.
Something abruptly stopped my fall,
a stony hand stood out
in the thickets of the night.
There a statue rose in the night dew
as if it were a solid chill of space.
The birds fell silent, only the wind
wheeled amidst the stars. Frightened, I looked
into the depth of his eyes and they were black undertows
devouring silence. Life stopped
as if I remained face to face
at the foot of foreboding. 'Who are you, lord of mist?
Perhaps the cliff of remorse,
or the unconfessable fear of what I know not?'
In the stillness, I felt his shadow
descend, dictating his law.

The World's Half-Shadow

The world's half-shadow places on my shoulders
all the distant weight of pain.
I tire. The world is slowly made of sorrow.
Oppressive dreams overwhelm me and hurt.
Dusks' clouded eyes
look no more, remain alone and age.

Like a grim avalanche, questions hurl down.
Facing the sheet of paper, I hear the impending
downpour's pattering, and the silence of smoke
rises above the darkened houses.
Unease and shadow. And the whisper
of the wind's wound slips through the cracks.

Towards the Mystery

On leaving the door of his room ajar,
he felt the breeze spread in its wings
a lively presence of colours:
blue and yellow butterflies,
mauve as the sea's remotest dreams.

They emerged from books, from photos and vignettes,
perhaps from a now confused terrain
enlarged by the wrinkles of melancholy.

He believed he won back the happy instants,
summer's best memories,
embers amid the willows and the tall galleon
cruising through the starry air.

Suddenly, a knot untying, the slow shiver
of everything that had been close to his heart,
and the sky a walnut size
boundlessly closed inside his fist
as though hiding from premonitions.

The fragrant window wafted in
the sea, the birches with stars in their crowns,
the memory of books that reread his soul,
beings and nights, worlds so rolling and alive.

There, too, were the favourite faces,
mirages of throbbing fire,
and, risen on the wind, the house of childhood,
poetry and its yearning arrow.

He felt once more the heart calling.
Never, never again, the hour told him,
while he slipped off alone towards the mystery.

from
Shiver
Escalofrío
(1999)

Conscience

You mean you no longer keep a strand of dreams
to reclaim your fate's lost inheritance?
You demand certainties, a fidelity
in keeping with the heart's peace,
free from forebodings where the defeated's
exhausted heartbeat appears.
How much scorn usurps your integrity.
Even in error you maintain, among mediocrities,
the pride of being the lord of wrecks.
Your eyes in the distant air
sculpted hope, the only possible
hope that ignores the rain of any misfortune.
It's difficult to last, to go on
insisting on a tenuous register of words,
hunting for them in half-shadowy years,
as if they saved or excused
this unease of deserving life.

Something Invisible Flows by Our Side

Perhaps to say good-bye to life
is to count the number of times we have left
to live in our warm customs.
Maybe these lukewarm quotidian things
offer the images of what they one day were:
proud encounters with the light,
or with that momentary mystery of beauty,
the voice of a woman, that poem,
a certain spellbound instant of dusk
when the air blazes on the balconies
and the valley, like a story, sleeps in its words.
Something remains latent on our lips,
a pleasure, an unease faced with the unspeakable,
and the breeze climbs the tower of jasmine
and whispers legends, slight insinuations.
Something invisible flows by our side,
a starry delirium, music from the cosmos
that throbs in its dazzled waiting.

The House at Skopje

Year after year I go back to a house in Skopje,
recover its bluish vistas
where clouds graze and my tense overwhelming
consciousness takes its plunge.
I pursue half-seen memories,
their dark sand banks, bonfires
bursting with shadows and fragrances
into the hidden depth of what I once was.

When I look at that diffuse sunset line
and the red shadow merges
with the past's convulsive embers,
what I feel is uncertain and near,
as if I beheld a vision of the future.

Astonishment wells up, sudden revelation
of a time still unborn.
Then I am a spellbound nomad,
the pale traveller arriving, throbbing
to know the truth, the emotion of his enigma.
The assembly of earth is what I reach
with its whiff of blood and roses' freshness.
Nothing in the world lives and is reflected
like that pure instant held
in the vibrant uneasiness of eyes,
outflowing in light, in song on the air,
to write the life I had and never had.

That's how my heart is, a pulsing of music,
a half-dreamed wine, my earthly joy.
I hear glasses of sincere friendship ring,
lights of affection quivering in crystal,

and I ride happily on the lightning,
on the red steed deserting death.
And I dream, laugh and speak, not knowing if I'm alive,
if I simply live on another level of time.

Perhaps it's this hand that felt the sky,
that one day invented deserts and gardens,
that yearns no doubt for a woman's body
and silently wrote the pain of its absence.
Its murmur confuses, in my memory revives
intense exposures beneath a starry ceiling
where an oasis paints its green eternity.

Thicknesses of Fright

I take refuge in the shadow my hands project,
as if I defended my frontier of dreams.
Something flashes within my eyes,
I glimpse in their frenetic signallings
grim thicknesses of fright.
Swarms of questions like insects,
like fierce harsh fireflies
whose light reaches me in all my exiles,
surrounding, blinding me with their avalanche.
I feel the meekness of mutilation
falling on the soul, scorching
the simple correlative of my story.
I grope the hostile night dew in the dusk
of tight words I cannot forget
and listen to the poem's winging
as if it were infinite space
hugging the solitary planet I am.

Resurrection

In mid-afternoon I am any old corpse,
and desire's a dune extending
into its own exile, its reservoir without ripples.
Not wanting to know, I don't even dream the landscape,
I ignore the territory dissected by the sunbeam
as if it were a skeleton in flight
from the mirage, a stone that anchored beneath silence.

Everything changes in the night. The stars reappear
from glittering polyhedrons. They are cats alert,
vehemently scratching a sun that became shadow.
Thirst stands up, growing with metaphors
from the deep heart's masts.
Here the enigma of forests sings,
the circle making your body feverish with mine:
slender high tide of full senses,
drunkenness and delirium of resurrection.

Your Heartbeat's Mine

And I struggled against dream and weariness,
against endless anger and uprootedness.
I searched, delved without an inkling of doubt
among blind faint embers
of my memory to find a year,
a solitary day, barely an instant
when I could say: I never loved you;
but I couldn't find a chink to lie to myself all alone,
to affirm even the slightest negation.
Your heartbeat's mine. There where that
acute desire we call life begins,
there, beaming in distant days,
in the blazing undergrowth of my astonishment,
with the yes and no of abyss or luck,
silently you wait like the tree of fire
holding that lustral fruit of hope.
My gaze invokes you in the present,
in the indecisive course of any distance
of that sea singing and seducing me
with lightning's vehement eyes.
You are the thirst of the Eden I don't perceive,
and in your voice's deep chords
you perennially remain, with the soul's
frozen music and daring springtime,
in every word of blood.

Sloth in its Wineskin

From all the mediocre, day emerges, swollen,
repeating its faces, gruff conversations,
debris of words rustling among the flies.

Loneliness under the sun, self-devouring abulia
from the indifference of a grim boredom
hiding its softness in half-shadow.

Behind the soul's veil a stray desire
chokes, insists on the sleepiness
of a discarded inertia, given over to scorn.

The look is sated with abandonment.
Any effort's useless and all resistance
an insult for idleness drowning in itself.

Confusion that doesn't listen to the decay,
nor to downfall's wind running deep
in the lying wineskin of sloth.

Calm Down

Frozen sunshade of sorrow,
why weep? Don't demand loyalty or nostalgia
of those who loved you. Don't look at your dead,
nor at the instant's empty branches,
nor at foolish words that never understand you.

Listen to yourself in the dawn wind,
in the sun that dazzlingly descends
to your heart to go on living.
Though you're alone, stand on your feet, never let
panic and failure leave you immobile.

Face your ghosts, they're your weary eyes'
pale guests. Once more, calm down,
let uneasy hours slip by
and think you're a lucky man
since you still kindle the light of your chimeras.

On the Threshold of Death

Your reality throbs within me.
I listen to you in confused thought,
as the one truth accompanying me to the end.
In your enigma, I foresee you visible.
From the first light at my side you were
like a lovely symbol of risk and rebellion.
Hieratic in your abyss, with the unknown's
tender attraction, you've been the greatest challenge.

Each day you combine better with my senses,
calm, reduce and silence them
on this strange threshold where you have me.
Patient, methodical, you ply your trade.
When I wake, I notice the clear cold
you've left on my skin, clouding my memories,
spilling in my mind the thirst for your substance.
Without you the ephemeral's refulgence would not exist,
nor the radiant intensity it uplifts,
nor would dreams be the fervour of the future.

In you silently advances the welcoming kingdom.
You are sculptor of the instant,
because of you, I call on earth, the greed of desire,
and even manage to believe you're God Himself;
for without your presence I would only be left
to live tediously without nostalgia or flame,
without the shadow of vertigo driving me to your core.

The Face of the Enigma

Suddenly I'm overwhelmed by the enigma of a face.
A fixed absolute face. Eyes where night
ascends and goes wild with the drumroll of wind,
where the moon with its seeding sprinkles
a wake of light thronging in my forehead.
This sudden murmur accompanying it belongs to the cold,
like wings reappearing from the cliffs,
crossing the dark while the eternal sinks.

Its breathing leads my existence
through dismal forests of a cruel defile,
an everlasting calendar with no answer.
An invisible blizzard. A nomadic gust.
In its unharmed universe appearances pulse.
Facing me its millennia are this one instant.

Its cheeks climb a space
of timeless darkness where chaos and origin
merge, succeed one another with unfeeling rhythm.
Its palate glitters with captive stars,
a subduing image revealing to all of us
it unanimous presence ringed with shadows,
the mouth engrossed in its sphere joins us
and, one by one, wipes us away in its silence,
without even grasping the pleasure of what's fleeting
or the punishment of being eternity.

Where Do the Dead Go?

Where do the dead go once snuffed out?
Into what infamous space will the pain descend
that doggedly reduces them, turning them
into the voices of the shadowiest wind?

From the dawning of tides
to the sirocco's desolate sands,
beneath pools and dunes, pebbles and out-jutting rocks,
I hear their delirious noises imprisoned
in the absent blindness of silence.

How to find the vigorous dream
to rescue them from their mirages?
That resolute dream that reaches the names
erased by ash to give the pulsing back
at last to their scorched minds.

Why do I imagine them on distant platforms,
lost and engrossed, beneath forgotten dates,
while dark rain shrouds and soaks them,
rots and scatters them away? Now weightless,
like dust or mist breaking up in air,
will they join the wind and rise in its heartbeats?

And how will they come back, in what trace or impulse,
from the stray unending of him who never returns?

Everlasting Night

Suddenly I opened my eyes in the mist –
black moon, huge blackboard, cliff –
and could see nothing. I felt memory
had forsaken me as well.

The city sucked in its exhausted desert,
as if the unfeeling darkness
had always filled its amorphous inexistence.

Reality emptied out my senses
towards swift slopes and drains,
falling in a gloomy stagnation
of invisible disowned objects.

I searched for my own shadow and that name,
but found language's awkward oblivion.
The voice became mist, a taciturn transparence.

Everything stayed in suspense and I went on through
the night of the soul like a rudderless boat without lights,
lost in phantom waters.

Night Waters of Delirium

Water of words, sounds that are voices
gushing from the heights, from the proud peak
of dream and dementia. Dizzy waters
falling in a great leap towards the void,
with the light of faces in each taut instant.
Faces that are beginnings, voices spells,
images, histories, years following one another
in the swift cascade of lives and time.

With that strength of the freest impulse,
with the constant fatality of night,
they exhaust, transcend one another in phosphorescence,
rising before sinking into the unknown.
Waters shaken with rage and pride
like hallucinations of a delirium of stars
amid clouds and beings of an exalted mirage.

Blue dazzling of space,
night surging in a frenzy of foam
towards territories burned by conscience.
It's the law of palpitating bodies,
magnetizing the power of their lust,
spelling the blazing name of desire.
It's the concealed current carrying
the passions of fire and its ashes
towards hidden hells of tears.

Incorruptible waters, waters of poppies,
flow on wings of forebodings,
on the terror of revelations
to purify our language.

Without the least pity, scarcely without knowing,
with their veil of mists, they shroud all memory.

Waters, swift faces of deadness, falling
from the eye's thick chambers
to the stray soul of oblivion.
Waters that were days, refulgent moments,
in the rich appearance of living
beneath the clarity of the created.

How will I return to the shore of the world?
Hands against the voices and their dizzying lights,
as if they still wanted to halt
the inevitable course of what's happened.
Hands under the slime, beheaded bodies,
nakedness divided, growing lost,
sinking down to the end, feeling the hatching,
the weight of nothingness in silence.

from

The Fire in the Diamond
(Sonnets)

El fuego en el diamante
(Sonetos)

1995–1998 (2000)

With You

With you in the sensual of harmony's way
beneath summer's cerulean light.
I bite into the cluster your open hands invite,
suck your carnal odour of midday.

I kiss your lips. You hush. You're mine.
I live the fullness of a human sea
raising proud surf gleefully
in the body of the man who craves your wine.

With you in the abyss that I foresee
and in desire carrying me away.
With you in the stars and wind run free,

making all it touches yours, mine throughout.
With you, all I am and feel I can be,
burning me in your eyes and in your mouth.

I Bite into the Peach

I bite into the peach. Its gold drips
by the teeth and flows into the throat.
Fresh pulp licking the sun, singing its note,
lighting up all that rings my lips.

Happy mouth that feels and spells
the longed for nectar and grows secure
in the thirst of a tongue lifting so pure
the smooth fullness of its tidal swells.

Now I drink this juice dissolved
in its coursing of aroma and caress.
It's the sensual instant when my hand

opens once more the fruit involved
to suck its flesh in delightful excess
of this radiant hour in summer's command.

Carnal Apple

Carnal apple, caressing moon,
heady clarity full of your fragrance
like a warm light finding entrance
to my skin, grows deep and dominant soon.

What impatient delirium the instant then.
My anxiety's a horseman who cannot tame
his steed, it's a wind, a dove lame
and wounded by a tragic diamond.

Your body is an oasis of lust,
a burning fountain that doesn't soothe the thrust
of thirst belonging to my secret desire.

You body's an abyss, a slow trap,
a cruel mirage without a firmament to aspire,
the endless crevice a mistake can map.

The Poet Speaks to the God of Silence

What am I in regard to you? That vanished
mote of dust, an atom, a tired
heartbeat in the chance of what life acquired,
hiding its penumbra, banished.

Why've you made me uneven facing nothingness?
To be a ghost unredeemed,
a game between the absurd and what the lost seemed,
confronting your ambush in my distress?

I swear I cannot understand you.
Here you leave me alone, condemned
to the useless punishment of the sonnet.

Here, disoriented, without having you,
almost blind, rebellious, my fortune requiemed,
unable to fathom your secret yet.

The Poor Devil

What shadow of hell mistreats me?
FRANCISCO DE QUEVEDO

What shadow of hell mistreats me?
From what vengeful God is the punishment
of having myself as my enemy to frequent
and being my own fire mortally to defeat me?

I'm the hurt by which I'm seized and tied
to the post of the torment I damn.
I am my hushed pain followed ad nauseam
in the faithless conviction by which I'm belied.

To stoke this fire blinding me
is anguish, agony and deep excess's friction.
To feel as pleasure my weeping alone,

to search in myself for what living denies me,
to sink the steely knife-edge of affliction,
with my own hands, down to the bone.

Now That I've Died, Let's See What Happens

Now that I've died, let's see what happens.
Where shall I go without blood or memory?
I am part of this shadow without history
that lies where a tabla rasa begins.

Barely cloudy air that burns
and goes astray in the invisible waterwheel
of that fleeting vainglorious feel
that was life, vocation, my house and concerns.

Someone orders what was mine erased,
but I don't want to stop being my master.
I face what still offers me a challenge.

I feel my body becoming a void enchased,
less than loneliness, dust and a dream's disaster,
in the slow thereafter of my agony's revenge.

from

The Forest of Nemi

El bosque de Nemi

1995–1999 (2000)

Summer Noon

This kind corner is what I want.
Here, among clover, beneath an acacia's
austere shade, listening to the cuckoo's song.
There's a huge happiness that comes from the breeze.
I make out the disquiet of tiny beings,
watching their flashing and their luck's chance.

I am reborn in the fleeting wind's flash,
surrounded by stones, by secret tracks,
feeling the caress of flowers
drinking, as I do, the noonday light.
I am enraptured by this never-changing landscape.
I watch the quivering pulse of its paths
with no other wink or course than life itself's.

What an ample underground fragrance
belongs to this bunch of violets with its starry mildness
bringing me memories of a distant heart.
Once more I am isolated, on indecisive days,
heeding words in which I hear
the trembling presences of seeds and birds.

Nothing calms eagerness and motion.
From his leafy balcony a green frog leaps.
Swallows arrive and make a sea of sky,
covering the air with feathery anchors.
Bumblebees drone by with their harsh engines.
The pine trees shiver like mirrors of sun.

The earthworm traces its sign in the clay.
The forest wellspring washes the hortensia's
slender feet and slips off to another meadow.

A snail unhurriedly crosses the grass
measuring the distances of summer.
June's linnet neatly prepares
its nest in the fork of a cherry tree.

Lively dragonflies launch their skimming flights,
rout the clouds of mosquitos and daddy-longlegs.
Suddenly a cicada intones his song.
Everything transports us to daydreaming's core,
there where myths are possible
and the fields fluctuate with lasting murmurs.

Narcissus

Narcissus was the light of beauty.
Slender and delicate as a lily,
he paused in his expression, lifted in his look
mystery's bottomless abyss.
It was hard to behold him without becoming
seduced by his splendour. He had a quality
that enveloped all, his unutterable
presence sprang from an intimate secret,
an essence of unachieved love.
It was a desire, an envisioned aura
that radiated unity with the expected.
Too subtle was its stimulating music,
its starry harmony with that unique shadow
that was and never was.
                         And one day it happened.
Hearing his heartbeat in the peace of a spring,
he saw a face pulse, watching him, entranced.
Oh, fatal beauty. He wanted to drink its lips
and didn't kiss its lips, drank a perennial water,
measureless love lost in a reflection,
an echo of life dreamed in its inside,
erased by the trembling waters.
Narcissus repeated: 'Come to me, come to me.'
And into the waters' depths he went to search
for the soul that flowed on in the current.

From that kiss, from that image wounded
by the slight touch of his lips,
only this winged flower remains that I offer you.

On a Nostalgic Cat

My cat was a wise self-absorbed fellow.
Genteel and distinguished, parsimonious,
as if day was the threshold of his kingdom,
he flowed towards night in his luxurious shadow
with immortality shining in his pupils.

He was a delicate friend, always agreeable
to any suggestion of my gestures.
And when he knew I was asleep and calm,
he climbed up to the roof balcony
to see the full moon and the constellations.

So, night after night, he pursued a mystery,
night after night he heard the silver heartbeat
of a strange presence brought by the breeze.
It was a sensual song, a light trill,
music from another time or maybe from another life
he barely remembered, when he was a bird.
What nostalgia in the air, what a blaze of celestial waves,
of blue flight and blinding feathers.

He dreamed again of being a shooting star,
green fire in the flash of lightning's wake.
Drunk with night light and absolute space,
quivering in the surprised abyss,
he went off to live in the song of a bird.

An Impossible Love

In the shadow's diffused light prolonging your body
I've seen your woman's shapes projected.
From the shoulders descends the solemn pillar
shaping the hips. They're so full and lovely
you seem to be sitting while you sink
your legs I cannot see into the vague horizon.

Where can you have lost your head?
I sense it in the dark with its Hellenic silhouette
so no one can sketch it,
so all of us can always dream it.
My fingers furrow your round amphora
and in your compact waves the sea is checked
and throbs with its greenest transparence.

Glitterings of stars in the night welcome you
and the fruit dish upholding you, naked and alone,
is now an unapproachable balcony.
I gaze at you in silence, bewitched
by you, pear, knowing your impossible love.

Pandora's Box

Pandora, in night's unredeemed blackness,
having found the place of the sacred box,
devoted herself to plotting, with a fickle mind,
the ambush of power and her strategy
with a single aim: to outwit
those capricious gods of Olympus.

Free and immune to the warning
of being a trap by the god Zeus
to affirm his breed against any human,
believing herself invulnerable without a doubt,
she opened the uncertain box.

A half-dark murmur
at the outset, later awful and confused,
in sudden surges went on imprisoning her.
A swarm of horrific creatures
called orphanhood, crime, madness, vice,
sickness, vengeance, plague, old age, misery
gradually overwhelmed the world of men.

Suddenly, from the depths of the box,
flew a butterfly with resplendent wings
that received the name of hope.
She taught man to maintain
his faith in love and desire
to be able to live without either.

Bellerophon and Pegasus

The god's immemorial voice rang out
in the gorge of dreams.
It rang reeling with love, with close tenderness.
Oh, come, Bellerophon,
spring up from the shadows of Corinth
so you can be a king's son
and the pride of a father living your adventure.

Like the light of boldness Bellerophon was born,
lovely as the sun among the waters,
beneath the marble ceiling and smiling.
He grew with a coin's strict appearance
and a powerful, chiselled body
that withstands torment and assails storms.
He lived beside eagles, was forged in silence.
Deserts and forests taught him
to watch for dangers, to go back to the law
of the strongest, as well as to survive
the ferocity of hunger and greed.

When the instant arrived which his long
and stubborn training had favoured,
he set out towards legend: the capture
of a winged mirage, the mythic Pegasus.
He felt the excess of his zeal.
It was to win over the wind's agility,
outdo the surf in violence,
lock up thunder and overpower lightning.
But he knew himself a man fulfilling his fate.

Invoking Athena, he directed his days
towards Mount Helicon in search of Pegasus.

He went through bramble hills, past cliffs and dales,
growing lost in mists and valley depths
where unmercifulness sharpened its teeth.
He was so exhausted he at last fell down worn out
near a stream with a speechless murmur.
When he fell asleep he suddenly noticed
a very bright, almost majestic vertigo.

From the air descended the shining whiteness.
His body was rippling, the face arrogant,
in his steady eyes fire flickered,
the energy and soul of the simoon.
Rebellious snowy manes shook.
Like proud unruly flags,
the clear, flashing wings,
showing the splendour of flanks.
The pure white hoofs like spears or stars
and a vibrant bonfire the upraised neck.

It was the solemn meeting of two singular looks.
Their eyes measured each other from before their origin.
They were stubbornness, spirit and courage,
stamping unruliness and rancor in flight.
They were the rebellion of furious passions,
each drinking in its unvarying mirror.
But, above all else, the thirst of victory
in both pounded in tendons and muscle.

Between his strong hands Bellerophon
tightened the bridles, the gold bridles given him
by the goddess. Unhesistant, he climbed on his croup.
The hoofs, the legs unleashed sparks
and earth thundered, wounded by his kicks.
Branches, rocks, pools shattered,
overcome by blows of lights and shadows.

Like winding forces that merge and split
amidst wind and mud, among trees and waters,
the faithful unrelenting enemies.

Like two comets enchased
that lit up night, the whole firmament,
with that same conviction and enigma
they twisted on themselves, one on the other,
pursued, fused fatally till they were,
in the vague form of their love,
the silhouette of a centaur emerging in half-shadow.

Perhaps Bellerophon was sure
of fufilling his spell, or in the depth
of his instinct, Pegasus understood
the useless struggle against a human being.
At last, beneath the light of simple understanding,
both horse and trainer
were left, after their effort, converted
into the lasting image crossing through space.

from

The Home Fire

Lumbre de hogar

1996–2000 (2000)

Sleeping Beside the Sea

Now you sleep with the breeze in the lazy night.
The heat of sultry weather wheels, dances sleepwalking
in the open murmur of the rooms.

Your breathing sculpts your senses.
Your heartbeats affirm your becalmed self.
Only the sea can be seen rough
in its shining shirking borders.

The water's splendour stretches your flesh.
A goddess of sun in your skin peeks out.
A radiant face whose gaze dreams
of the bluish fire of twinkling stars.

What to say about your lips, honey of an aura
where spring is enslaved.
Neck of snow and fire, dreamed by the brume
of white birches and Nordic spaces.

Swans are the heralds of your shoulders,
and in their light fall towards height,
breasts of demented light, surprised
in the hidden modesty of their delicateness.

From your waist the time of oasis is born,
the bewitched music of a visible mystery.
In its weightless caress wakes the garden
of the most intimate temple. There pulses
the one pleasure that makes us innocent.

Your Crystalline Space

What waters and skies you open in your girlish eyes
when you look at me, how much light you shed
to walk and find me in my heart,
engrossed in it, and make me your own.

In your gaze, I forget the stars,
your voice is made of rainbow crystal,
a whisper floating on the fragrance
of streams of dreamy purity.

You come from some heavenly unending, from some
flowery season where innocence is born
and the wheat-white day dons colours
to set your hands alight and the air you caress.

Pollen of tenderness, you are warm snow,
smooth as the glistening of dew,
steady as hope's heartbeat
where the future writes its loveliest song.

When you still did not exist, the murmur of forests
and freshness of the breeze in the sunset
brought your memory from a sun of orange blossoms,
spurring me to believe once more in miracles.

I sowed you in the brightest place of my dream,
and so, in the green wake of one night, you arrived
to affirm your crystalline space
with this fullness offered me by your life.

From You I Hope for Everything

Lara, wise little one, who still doesn't know how to speak.
From you I expect everything, I mean, the time
of ripe and happy years.
Those that show me true infancy,
where once more the heart dreams
like a god explaining his mystery.

When I'm old, and you in the fullness of youth,
you must take me over summer's paths,
knowing I receive the world through your eyes
and trust the peace of my conscience to your kindness.

Tell me, Lara, what've you done with my time,
with my urge to express the instant's essence
and protagonize my own story?
I know this love for you is part of the enigma
that, in each life, comes into existence,
and renews the miracle of being in another being,
blinding the desolate questions.

A Fable for When You're Gone

After they forgot you, you've not grown old again.
The days go by, mother, and, seeing you in my memory,
I have a feeling your eyes are greener. Your long hair
so blonde attains the clear sheen
of the sun's smooth images.
Today, as yesterday, I poured clean water on your flowers.
Now nothing wounds me or offends.
Now I am older than you and wearier.
I, too, grew used to talking alone
with my faithful absences and new pains.
I go on being bewitched by the cicadas' sound.
I still have not lost
this dreamy light in my eyes. I accept being here,
reduced, silent, confined,
till one day I'll forget
the road back from dreams,
to be at last your song,
part of the air, fire living in your gaze.

The Oneness of Life

When one day the fields are blindness and night,
and broad springtime just a forgotten name,
I'll head back to the pulse of light.
I'll come like the clouds that flow in the dawn,
hoping to be rain and later seed
thrusting through the clay. I shall be born,
I'll tear apart a silence of fire, earth or water.
I'll blaze in impatience, climb through the air
with the tender equilibrium of a flame.
It will be like beginning to grow anew,
running hurriedly through the grass,
suddenly embracing the surprise of water
and the spikenards' passionate perfume.
I'll feel the delight of the forest listening,
the touch of sky in my pupils,
the lips pronouncing the word.
All the love of star-studded space
I'll win all at once in that instant
when once more I come back to existence,
to its fervent oneness and miracle.

from

Sketches in a Parenthesis
(Poems Not Included in Books)

Trazos en un paréntesis
(Poemas no recogidos en libros)

1965–2000 (2000)

Borges

(HOMAGE ON HIS CENTENARY)

You made, from darkness, simple light,
interpreted the dream of history,
the sagas' glow, the memory
of Isidoro Acevedo and his seed's plight.

You knew the fragile wonder
in the constant roll of your water wheel,
the humanity and vainness of glory's appeal:
a tragic fate letting no light linger.

Of all the miracles and sin,
no doubt you longed for the luckless man's skin
that crossed the Eden of the disperse.

You knew no action, but knew its adventure,
snatched the flame from the depths' lure
and, blindly, you unveiled the universe.

Signs of Exile

The professor, with a peerless expression
of cold, blessed prima donna,
preening his voice, gazed on his hordes
of Aeolian buttocksmen seers
and pointed to the void: 'If you love me,
you should steadily silence him.
He's dared to usurp the unusurpable,
an instant of glory that belonged to me.'
The docile acolytes lowered their foreheads
and a collective stench of general repugnance
went down the rungs of promotion ladders:
'That wicked one went astray, let's condemn him,
open him a desert, wipe out his word.'

The order was carried out, but the forsaken fellow,
ay, kept on, unharmed, lighting up his verse
throughout every corner of the earth.

Shoes for Death

Death will one day have my shoes.

In the end, she's always a mother, sinister,
who'll know how to wait for me with punctual fury.
Maybe, for a second, I was born from her forgetting.
That remorse doesn't want to leave her,
must always mortify her in her greed
of tedium, cold stone and inconclusive ash.

That's why, when looking at my empty shoes,
my death accuses them for supporting me,
and, hateful, promises them one day I'll have to leave them.

No doubt they cause in me a certain pity.
Injured, they listen and protect me
from mud and rain, from the insatiable desire
of this stubborn mother insisting in my shoe soles
on dragging me towards slime and silence.

In the Deaf Man's Country House

HOMAGE TO GOYA

In the unfathomed sea of voiceless days
a hell in the soul is my deafness.
It emerges from desolate winds,
making itself a landscape where mud flats die.
My eyes are now burning craters
from fury's white-hot splinter.
I painted worlds and degrading courts,
granted life to bodies lit
by a dark lust's convulsive terror.
I penetrated into the deepest core of Satanic looks,
searching for the way to devour my dreams.
Grapes of disappointment, I listen to you rain down
with my country's bloodstained lament.
A helpless century lost in its dementia.
I belong to myself no more, I am this harsh night
hanging in the noose of all my exiles.
With awful colours, I have to invent
the torn voices I cannot reach,
exorcize the spurious, hearing the infamies
that cruelly pursue me through foolish penumbras
of black daybreaks. Under the earth
of silence, like underground water,
I still howl and damn, I am this whirlwind,
the most desperate one thrashing on the canvas,
foreboding the appalling future of man.

Twentieth Century

You go down to your grave, Twentieth Century,
with your pain and night raining upon you
as if our blood foresook
the worn-out echo of your history.
From sunset's cloud of dust
where a light of fog settles,
angry crowds emerge from the abyss.

Grim generations come, disappear
with the same disorder as the sea's and its wrecks.
Its rebellion dies out like a cry
in the dark prison of impotence.
They arrive from chaos itself with misery and hunger,
listening to the death-rattles of a dying star
on the earth inhabited by dishonour.

The threat hovers round every day.
Genocide weapons that created your wars,
aim at us, ready to raise
the gigantic mushrooms poisoning the airs,
making us premature shrouds,
helpless skins beneath the typhoon of fire.

Twentieth Century, your acts hoard the pestilence
etched in the soul of those who still resist.
The vile suffering of the disinherited
put out your untenable prestige,
not knowing what we still call harmony.

Confused, you dissolve on the stones of the moon,
in greenery scorched by the wind's leprosy,
extinguishing the slender suns of wellsprings

with aching unmercifulness, without shocks,
forgetting the heartbeat of existence,
to fall in the end before my eyes
like a curtain scattering your ashes.

A PASSION FOR REMEMBRANCE:
THE POETRY OF JUSTO JORGE PADRÓN

JUSTO JORGE PADRÓN belongs to the second stage of a group of poets whose first wave was the so-called 'Venetians' or 'culturalists' dating from *Arde el mar* ('The Sea Blazes', 1966) by Pere Gimferrer, a poet who has now become a significant figure in Catalan poetry. Two outstanding poets of the second wave are Antonio Colinas and Jaime Siles. Colinas continued the culturalist style of the early work of Guillermo Carnero by using the dramatic monologue of an historical figure when he was not waxing languid and sensual in the ruins of classical culture, though some of his more recent work takes a cosmic turn, pondering the 'starry void'. The intellectual Jaime Siles develops poetic thought in sensuous form. Padrón, however, is more varied and fitful than either of these two and his work does not share the aesthetic distancing characteristic of the culturalists. He can be apparently neo-romantic like Colinas, but his poetry essentially derives from personal experience and, in this aspect, occasionally recalls the meditative lyricism of Francisco Brines, a poet of the 1950s. Padrón's second book is dedicated to him. If for Brines time inevitably leads to death and nothingness, a condition he accepts with stoic fatalism, Padrón's perspective is more disturbing and cosmic in its searching. Time is also the destroyer for Padrón, but his poetry emerges from the contest between visions of a black future and dreams of salvation in a woman's arms or in nature's restive, and sometimes ideal, beauty. His poems vary from hope to desolation according to the obsession of his mood. The grimness of death may be present but is attenuated by the exaltation and refuge of oneiric flights.

Justo Jorge's first published book *Los oscuros fuegos* ('The Dark Fires', 1971; Second Prize in the Adonais Awards of 1970), with its oxymoron of life's intensity including its extinction, refers to the ardour of experience and the nocturnal pallor of its recollection. Memories of love are tinged with a sense of failure based on loneliness, lost passion and the drudgery of working days. Poems of domestic tenderness contrast with the hostile city and its 'mirrors without mercury', a prefiguring of a more surreal use of mirrors in *The Circles of Hell*. Padrón's second book, *Mar de la noche* ('Sea of the Night', 1973; Boscán Award, 1972) presents a more disturbing transcendence into a world of uncertainty where hallucinations oversee reality. The remembered sensations of youth give way to life as an implacable passage to a sea of doubts pounding the hopes of man. The poet's fears in one poem are reflected in surrounding eyes that shed no forgiveness. Another text speaks of 'a lonely and incurable desire' and 'a passion created by death / With a radiance more beautiful than life'. Such texts presage the dark, compulsive side of Padrón's poetic personality.

This grim aspect of a visionary loss of identity in a loveless, hostile world unfolds in its most extreme form in Justo Jorge's most renowned work, translated into more than thirty languages, *Los círculos del infierno* ('The Circles of Hell', 1976; Swedish Writers' Association Award for the best European book of poems for 1976; Fastenrath Award of the Spanish Royal Academy, 1977). Based on the idea of the poet as Everyman, the work begins with 'The Invasion of the Atoms', in which 'A suicidal planet' bursts inside us, an explosion imagined as atomic destruction. The borders between inward self and external reality are intentionally blurred to take on the hurt of a wounded world in dream-inspired imagery. It ends with a labyrinthine vision of death itself as the poet sinks into the darkness where

> The dead keep falling from rivers and tombs,
> From nights and crimes and forgotten centuries,
> Revolving towers of eyes and rigid faces [. . .]

One is reminded of the 'vertical river of the dead' in 'Only Death' by the Chilean poet Pablo Neruda (1904–1973), but Padrón's is not death as a journey upstream but an irreversible descent into the depths of the ocean with reality being 'no noise, no sign, / No voice, no silence'. Only in the second section does the poet offer the relief of sensual woman, the magic of infancy and the house as a home redeemed by the birch tree and stars. Perhaps because of the mirrors as chasms of the self in the final section, Spanish Nobel Laureate Vicente Aleixandre (1898–1984) referred to this book as 'an imprisoning symbol of man's fate'.

The catastrophic sense of reality in *The Circles of Hell* receives a peaceful, serene contrast in *El abedúl en llamas* ('The Birch Tree in Flames', 1978). In an austere idyll amidst the natural setting of Scandinavia, Padrón heals the crisis-sensibility of his previous work with brief vignettes of nature in which he develops a fresh facet of his poetic resources, which he calls 'The diaphanous craft / Of a minute art'. He turns his precision of word and metaphoric imagination on various elements, water, sea, birch tree, the flora and fauna of northern summers to extract images of beauty. Though there is an occasional note of gloom – the last verse refers to 'a dark impulse of hate or death' – the book's spiritual goal is 'renunciation and light', a search for permanence in the passing seasons. A drop of dew can become a kindled planet as the poet links the minuscule and the grandiose. Remembered loves and personalities add to the work's tone of reverie. Two poems stand out: a tribute to Mexican poet and critic Octavio Paz as a tamer of the animals of the imagination, and an evocation of the aurora borealis in Iceland which gives delirious rein to the Canary Island poet's associative abilities with their 'Music staffs, sails, flags, / Embers and flowers of the locked light'.

Otesnita (1979), Justo Jorge's fifth book, is a name invented by the poet to designate his beloved and her aura of tenderness and natural beauty. Like a diptych, the work presents the ecstatic emotion of an ode to a love affair, and an elegy of desolate loss as disappointment sets in. As often with Padrón, deep emotion vies between delighted enthrallment and apprehensive despair. Love becomes a telluric goal, but it also a fire with its attendant ashes. The story is told in terms of imagery from nature, so a seagull's apparently immobile flight is transformed into 'a tear searching for a face'.

Padrón's next two works were published together in 1984, *La visita del mar* ('The Sea's Visit') and *Los dones de la tierra*

('The Gifts of Earth'). *The Sea's Visit* represents a crossroads in Padrón's poetic development as it allows him to develop both his metaphorical abilities in a natural context as well as his apprehension of ageing and death as an inevitable future, his Apollonian sense of harmony between man and nature and his Dionysian intuition of death's destruction. The three sections of the book, which correspond to day, dusk and night, illustrate the journey of a man's life from hope and vitality, through fear and doubt, to a final awareness of death's grim presence as a final solution. In the first part, the sense of wonder at nature ranges from descriptions of the rooster's call, the hawk's flight and the tiger's stalking to the immersion in the sea of thought that brings up names on the blank page and the visit of Neptune in his hoary splendour. In the second part, fear and loneliness command, as in 'Night in the Cry', an example of what Spanish poet and critic Carlos Bousoño calls 'the proliferating image' where a single idea or noun spurs the imagination through the rest of the poem. In this context of middle age, the word is no longer name-giving and creative but imprisoning and potentially poisonous. In the final section, the poet rows in deep waters until a final poem recalling the holocaustal images of *The Circles of Hell*, in which the individual's disappearance becomes an onslaught of corrosive tears from the heavens, an image based on Italian poet Cesare Pavese's notion that death will come and have your eyes.

The Gifts of Earth seeks relief from personal concerns in lyric descriptions of the four elements of earth, air, fire and water. Just as Neruda and Aleixandre dealt with elemental things in their poetry, Padrón describes the human alliance with substances that were the origin of life for pre-Socratic philosophers. Joining the familiar with the mysterious, he sees the sea finally as 'sheer light / Of a God inhabiting us forever'.

THE PRESENT anthology represents both a widening and deepening of the topics found in *On the Cutting Edge*. The island boy who threw a stone in the water is still seeing the reverberations in his work. Every poet, in some sense, repeats and embellishes his first writings, but in Padrón's case, we can see definite pairings. His most successful book, *The Circles of Hell*, now has a mate in *The Radiance of Hate*. In this case, the breadth of the earlier book, in which self-loathing and Kafka-esque diminishment could be expanded to include atomic destruction and visionary extremes, is more directly approached as the self-incarnation of human hate developed in similes such as the black drop or the ice of a name till it turns Christian virtue on its head in a parody of the Lord's Prayer.

The structure of *The Sea's Visit*, which includes a number of poems that were not about the sea at all, expands to include two concerns in Padrón's poetry: one illustrated by a book about the sea, *Embers of Nadir*, in four moments of its varied day, 'Night', 'Morning', 'Noon' and 'Dusk'; the other, based on the three section titles of *The Sea's Visit*, 'The Gardens of the Sun (Morning)', 'The Losing Years (Afternoon)' and 'Fears of Death (Night)', serves as the source for the five sections of two of his more recent books, *A Whisper of Agony* and *Shiver*. The gardens of sun and sensuality are not so prevalent in these books, but the idea of losing years and fears of death are fundamental in them, for Padrón's basic procedure in most of his books is to consider each one as a disturbing journey through life with death as a presence or veiled threat. A revealing poem called 'The Poet's Maze' from *A Whisper of Agony* quite simply begins 'The doubt of being or perhaps not being.' Cuban writer Virgilio López Lemus, borrowing a poem title from *Shiver*, calls his book on Padrón's poetry *Eros y Thanatos* (Madrid: Verbum, 2002), for indeed love and destruction are constants in his lyrics. However, in these last two books, we can speak of the Heideggerian theme of *Dasein*, human life or 'Being-in-the-world', as 'Being-towards-one's-own-death' (*Sein zum Tode*). Death as the potentiality of human life can be found as early as Padrón's second book, *Sea of the Night*, in 'The Burning Wave Sweeps You Along' where even the poet's house 'Stops being the one refuge / Against death'. The poet's visionary wave of the world's scum drives him to flee his surroundings even as he cannot escape the consciousness of his own mortality. Likewise, the erotic death wish shows up in 'If Just Once' from the poet's first book, *The Dark*

Fires, for 'The heart revives / When singing in the limits of the lover', and that passionate heart 'prefers death before exodus, / Because to leave – stone said so before – is to die, / To fertilize forgetting'. Being in love is the true form of life; living without it or even with its memory is suffused with an immanence of extinction.

The same notion of each book of poetry as almost an allegorical passage through love's delights, a period of pain and an adumbration of death can be found in Padrón's book of sonnets, as the section titles themselves suggest: 'On Love and Its Fire', 'The Endless Crevice', 'The Pain and the Delirium', 'The Shadows of Death'. There is a strong sense of drama in the hyperboles of this perspective, but never a whiff of sentimentality. Rather it is the concentration of Padrón's alternatives, the fusion of love and nature mixed with the impending threat of death that makes the Canary Island poet such an arresting lyric personality. The lyric poet feasts on strong emotions: 'Welcome joy, and welcome sorrow', Keats wrote, and this swing from one extreme of feeling to another, mixed with a pure sense of wonderment at Nature and human nature, characterizes Justo Jorge's dimensions of the poetic.

MEMORY OF THE FIRE opens with a surprise selection from what actually turns out to be Justo Jorge Padrón's very first book of poems. In an interesting introduction to his collected poems, 'Poetry as Fate', he writes that he owes his literary vocation to the chance moving of a group of books which fell on the floor, leaving one damaged, the novel *Pan* by the Norwegian writer Knut Hamsun (1859–1952), which whetted his appetite for Nordic literature. By the time he was twenty he had written a first notebook of poems, which he never published, and later finished a first book that was to be published in the discontinued San Borondón list. For three decades – from 1966 to 1996 – *Escrito en el agua* ('Writ in Water') remained unpublished. Though its poems may lack the development of later works, the book has a freshness that comes from the awakening of love, one could almost say a consecration of desire and sensual yearning. At the same time, poetry is personified in the figure of a woman, and Keats' epitaph is taken to mean that the word maintains a timeless autonomy, even though the poet's name may be erased in water. Sensual love becomes an objective correlative for faith in life, so the loved one may even be a 'Little church in which to pray to God'. 'Night of the Invisible' indicates how Padrón's ear is tuned to the night, to the voices of the unknown in a constant search for intimations of the cosmic.

Sólo muere la mano que te escribe ('Only the Hand That Writes You Dies', 1989), from which samples appeared in the previous English anthology, was published together with *Los rostros escuchados* ('Heard Faces'). Originally conceived as one book, the first title was expanded to deal with the notion of meta-poetry, that which is concerned with itself and with the relationship between the word and the external world it contains. The title poem conceives of poetry as a beautiful woman and how the text written to her makes her last. To some extent, the poet's personality becomes embodied in the written search for meaning. The builder of signs with his Promethean instinct steals not fire but the word to give his verbal searching glimpses of the immortal. Personification leads the poet to conceive the word as his experiential body and the tundra as the primal landscape whose whispers spur the fire of creativity. If the word was made flesh in the gospel of St. John, the poet in 'The Seething Setting' plays on the analogies between pen and paper and the natural world which the poem suggests or creates in order to establish a personal, lyric world. The poet's reaching out to incorporate the stars in 'Like a White-Hot Loom' leaves him with the longing to have the stars' 'shadowy sails' coursing in his blood.

Heard Faces begins as the previous work ended, on a cosmic note, with the night sky as the air's aquarium, perhaps inhabited by the speaking faces of the poet's past as a synaesthetic confirmation of friendship and generation, but the first of the book's five parts summarizes a variety of themes, from the youthful poet's blood pact with the birch tree's sap to the vision of lost loves as so many oysters of experience gulped down. In addition, we find hell as a family quarrel. The second section, 'The Pebbles of the Cold', details, often in an epigrammatic style, the desolation of desire that can lead to visions of the alien city and impending death. The third part, 'The Snail and His Smile', includes texts with a whimsical humour devoted to small creatures, apart from the snail, the louse, fleas and the cat. Yet it also contains poems that take place in the time of the eternal, when the poet has orders to be born, when he sees a cosmic girl juggling oranges that become comets, or when he imagines a wager between one whom Justo refers to in his introduction as 'the human God that protected our ancestral past' who loses to 'a new God who currently rules over us'. The loser becomes an insignificant being called Adam. The fourth section deals with the poet's Grand Canary Island setting, most notably in 'Mount Lentiscal', where the poet's family home is located, but nature also includes the memory of lost love. This theme, in the last section, leads to some of Padrón's most memorable recollections of love and its errors, the chimera of desire and the permanence of longing.

Resplandor del odio ('The Radiance of Hate', 1993) returns to the controlled insanity of the lyric protagonist who traps himself in the desert hell of his own making – this time, not the ego as everyman as in *The Circles of Hell*, but as the damned and the infamous. If *The Circles of Hell* influenced the passive poet, this work has the poetic ego involved in demonic self-destruction by maintaining his hate of others. A whole book largely dedicated to hate is essentially a field trip for the negative shadow of the unconscious. Yet the others as enemies are intentionally left blurred so that the black drop of memory turns on itself to become an 'emptiness blowing itself away'. In the process, the Christian 'Our Father' is turned on its head to support man's revenge against himself. Hate turns into the devil in this fragmented lyric psychodrama. If Lucifer in *Cain* (1821) by Lord Byron declares to the murderous brother that he will not say 'Believe in *me* as a conditional creed / To save thee', the subversion of Christian language in the second part of *The Radiance of Hate* depends on accepting this emotion as a kind of Anti-God. So 'Creed' intones: 'I believe in almighty hate, / Creator of its shadow and its own threat', turning this power against itself.

The poem that closes the book offers a homage to Thomas de Quincey who published his essay 'Murder Considered as One of the Fine Arts' (1827), with the intention stated in his epilogue of skirting the edge of horror and everything whose concrete realization would be highly repulsive. Padrón shares this objective, and as the English author mentions the rattlesnake eye of the murderer and the Medusa head of another character, the Canary Islander develops these themes in poems, but he emphasizes that the lyric self in the throes of hate is a victim of his own vengeance, locked in the circle of his own hell. Female sexuality offers respite in this work, as it did in *The Circles of Hell*, but the references to animals and insects reminds us that Todorov, in his *Introduction à la littérature fantastique* (1970), declared that the existence of beings more powerful than man is a constant of this kind of literature.

If a certain anxiety and unfulfilled desire seems to spur Justo Jorge's imagination, just as *The Circles of Hell* was followed by a largely serene work like *The Birch Tree in Flames*, *The Radiance of Hate* is soothed by *Manantial de las presencias* ('The Wellspring of Presences', 1994, Guadalajara Province Award). Clarity itself becomes a topic in the description of a sunbeam, and domestic harmony, fugitively found in *The Dark Fires*, reappears in evocations of the poet's parents or in appreciations of daily things like wine, coffee and the peach, even Adam's discovery of poetry. The book's four parts include a two-part interlude dedicated to Mozart as an evocator of nature and a joyous harbinger of musical light. Poetry, all it does, its relationship with dreams and words as inscrutable signs, makes up the third part, while the final section concentrates on the contents of poetic consciousness, even its warlike phantoms and its strange hallucinatory wall of 'feverish histories', and includes a tribute to Spanish political cartoonist Mingote as also a creator of visions. Perhaps *Wellspring of Presences* illustrates Padrón's idea, expressed in his introduction, that the poet who breathes fully in his work is 'protean. His forms are as varied as his changing nature'. Yet he also names three elements that he especially loves: the sea, the forest and the stars.

This last element is the basis for Justo Jorge's next book, *Oasis de un cosmos* ('Oasis of a Cosmos', 1994). 'The Eyes of the Night' from *The Circles of Hell* and 'Like a White-Hot Loom' from *Only the Hand That Writes You Dies*, with the stars that speak to the poet in his enigmas, are precedents for this type of poem. The temperate, subtropical climate of Grand Canary Island surrounded by the Atlantic Ocean may make the poet more aware of the night sky than an inland city poet would be. In any case, the stars as 'Blinking magma of invisible volcanoes' means that he has the volcanic Canary Islands in mind. As is often the case with a large limiting natural phenomenon, the associative possibilities for metaphor and simile are manifold, so he reads the microcosmos into the macrocosmos and sees 'windows in flames', the house of heaven. He can imagine everything from trees to luckless warriors battling in eternal strife without human pity, or he can impose the comfort of a peaceful landscape on the firmament's breadth. Human loneliness can be projected into a star and a rose can recall starry qualities. Finally, the stars may suggest their invisible creator, insinuate an indecipherable voice, suggest a human plea, remind man he is a mote of dust but still make him believe that starlight somehow seems part of the substance of his blood.

Ascuas del nadir ('Embers of Nadir', 1995), which won a prize in the International City of Las Palmas Awards, brings the same kind of imagination to bear on another vast natural phenomenon, the sea in four moods of a single day, but this time 'the tremulous throbbing of the abyss' leads the poet into a more chaotic, and possibly even more creative, vision of natural power than he found in the stars. Whether horses, fire or battalions, the briny depths bring out the best in the Island poet. Some aspects of language and theme in Padrón's poem recall section XIV, 'The Great Ocean', from the *Canto general* ('Universal Song', 1950) by the great Chilean poet, Pablo Neruda. In the case of Padrón, the sea is the foundation of his poem, speaks to him in the first part and, in the final, grants him 'the vibrant genesis of language / from its prophecy of horizons'. Both poets use the drop of water as a synecdoche for the whole, but Padrón emphasizes the sea's redemptive aspect: 'Drop that saves the world, lifts and purifies it'.

Justo Jorge's ocean becomes a proving ground for what Joseph Campbell in *The Hero with a Thousand Faces* (1949) calls the 'monomyth', the hero who faces the dangers of darkness and abyss to return to humanity with new knowledge; in the case of the poet, with the poetic word. The archetypal adventure of universal man represents the basic hope of human beings to explore their origins and come to terms with them and with their mortal limitations. Campbell divides the monomyth into three stages: the separation or departure, the trials and victories of the initiation, and the return and reintegration into society. Out of the four temporal sections of *Embers of Nadir*, the first two, 'Night' and 'Morning', correspond to the setting out, the falling into a submarine underworld, the experience of the sea's chaos; 'Noon' refers to the trial, though the text suggests the erotic daydream in the sea (possibly Carl Jung's version of the Primal Mother) and the encounter with the creatures of the deep; 'Dusk' represents the return to society, though it may be a kind of farewell to former friends and a praise of friendship. In the third section, it becomes clear that the poet searches for something to release him from 'The oblivion of so much empty fatality' and he hopes to come back with fresh understanding: 'Will a new order be born, a greedy present, / The lasting conscience beyond the ruin?' *Embers of Nadir* weds the prodigious imaginative powers of the poet to a narrative of Everyman who searches for answers and finds inklings of order in the vast canvas of nature. Padrón's introduction to his collected poems indicates that he considers it his 'best and most ambitious poem'.

In the logic of Padrón's lyricism, a book that ends so positively as to have the poet leaving his verses on the sea's shore 'Like a lasting emblem of what sings and lives' should be followed by a swing back to the darker side of his poetic reality. In the introduction referred to, he offers several ideas about his poetics. Literary experience has shown him that:

poetry is an infinite polyhedron and in each one of its facets dizzy and changeable reality can be seen reflected. And given that man has no centre of gravity in himself, we can say that the poem is his pendulum, the compass that orients him towards the incorruptible home of dreams. Poetry is the only art that gives light and colour to that dark house that is the world. She is the one that keeps the language of those humbled by pain. Poetry is not a simple attribute of the poem but a hidden symbol of what exists.

Indeed, Padrón claims that poetry 'is more than reality' insofar as 'it is a reality that expresses and transcends itself' to see the invisible and express 'an individual cosmogony', a theory of the universe. His following book, *Rumor de la agonía* ('A Whisper of Agony', 1996; City of Las Palmas International Award, 1995), however, does not imply so much the surrealistic break-up of a personal world as in *The Circles of Hell* or an extreme emotion such as *The Radiance of Hate*, but rather a controlled reflection on the presence of death in daily life, vitality bereft of its consolations and focused on its coming extinction. A grim austerity rules over this volume, a laconic look at the obverse side of life in which hope cannot be reinforced by 'the bile of dreams'. The poet who thinks his ironic smile can dupe misfortune is accosted by old age, and images of rain again, as in other books, proclaim the ruin, yet paradoxically he wants to see that rain as part of 'a long monologue claimed by oblivion'.

A Whisper of Agony takes a wizened view of love, not as life-enhancing, but as truncated by time or marred by the agony of its enforced battle of sensuality and desperation, for the beloved's gaze lends not its own reward, but 'eternity that dies'. An emptiness sets in throughout the five parts of the book so that symptoms of human night darken the possibility of reverie and leave man pondering the wound of his abyss of fear and foreboding. Life is drained by a consideration of its ending. The pain of being and travelling to its own death in a boat of insomnia leaves the heart pondering the omens of its subtraction as the enigma of being.

With *Escalofrío* ('Shiver', 1999; Barcelona Poetry Reading Prize, 1998), Padrón once more explores the presence of death, but this time with a greater sense of the vital contrast offered by love's recollection. Reacting to the feeling of threatened existence in the previous book, *Shiver* goes so far as to present 'Life like a beloved, dazzling woman', but the sense of transgression sharpens the Luciferian conflict of self seen in the mirror as a kind of *doppelgänger* dialogue between Eros and Thanatos, with the only victory that of silence and nothingness. In this context the claims of love are magnified to resurrection and a kind of Eden doomed to fail in a contrasting sense of love's destructive force. In the five sections of the book, the first two, 'Irrepressible Blood' and 'Love Chooses its Path', are countered by the numbing loneliness of life's journey in 'Years of Renunciation', 'The Greed of Time' and 'The Expanse of Death'. The renunciation becomes a sandstorm image of the body's anonymity. Pain blinds and writing's support, paper itself, becomes imprisoning as hope declines. As in *A Whisper of Agony*, the last two sections of *Shiver* deal with death in life, either the low tide or desert or snow which living suggests to the poet. Padrón finally personifies death as an enticing lover, though the poet's delirium mixes memories and desire in amputating waters and final silence.

El fuego en el diamante ('The Fire in the Diamond', 1995–1998, published 2000) adds a new dimension to Padrón's lyric endeavour, a book of sonnets that also explores the human trajectory from love to pain to impending death as the four section titles indicate: 'On Love and its Fire', 'The Endless Crevice', 'Pain and Delirium' and 'The Shadows of Death'. The first praises the sonnet form for its intensity of life, and then describes the beloved in her nakedness and portrays love as admiration, linking the loved one to sea, rain, spring, river, bonfire and the mirror for its transparence. What the poet extols is a 'goddess at home'. The second introduces desire's temptation in which the body of the beloved is a wound and an abyss and the poet is pursued by a hidden enemy of bitterness. But if love also entails anguish and the remorse of 'dead loves' taken away by time, their recollection is a form of light.

The third section questions the meaning of life in an atmosphere of undefined dread, sorrow is found in joy, and memory, failing, grows into forgetting. In the autumn of life, the poet speaks to the god of silence and considers the self as enemy. In the final part, life is seen as a cut flower, and the lyric ego is plagued by a herald of foreboding, feels himself as an outcast and finds a murderous claw in the soul as he tries to contemplate what afterlife may follow his agony in the imagined void.

With *El bosque de Nemi* ('The Forest of Nemi', 1995–1999, published 2000), Padrón presents the forest as a kind of lost paradise for the recreation of myth and the exaltation of nature. The book inherits some of the delicate imagery of *The Birch Tree in Flames*, but the poems are more elaborate, and represent a more sustained play of the imagination. Nemi is a forest 'where dreams live' and these include naiads, an imagined sea and the forest as a series of masts. The poet portrays the woodland at different times of the day and he is visited by angels and even the fallen angel. The whole is ruled by 'crystal laws' and human emotions are bestowed on everything from trees to black rocks, from the river personified to the life of the nameless flower. On the one hand, Padrón conceives the apple as a woman, on the other, he has the bluebottle tell of his failed union with the divine. Natural elements are eroticized, such as the trembling poplar that pursued a dryad. Familiar Greek and Roman myths are retold or alluded to. The poet makes a pact with Dedalus to recreate his flight, and he listens to the god of words incite him to write his lines to stave off death. Pandora opens the box of troubles for mankind but also lends him hope. A wonderful tribute to Aphrodite's breasts is countered by a portrayal of Jupiter, as a demoted god, trivialized in a tourist image or left as a broken statue urinated on by dogs. The light of love speaks to the lyric self till, at length, he realizes that the forest itself is all one metonym for the poet's heart still trying to save him.

Lumbre de hogar ('The Home Fire', 1996–2000, published 2000) represents the most sustained exercise of tenderness and poetic feeling for the poet's family surroundings to be

214

found in his work. Dedicated to his daughter Lara, born 1st January 1997, the book comprises a number of poems dedicated to her as though she were a gift of existence given to a blind man, one renewing 'the miracle of being in another being, / Blinding the desolate questions'. In addition, it includes texts dedicated to his wife's beauty and his love for her, poems to his mother and sister and even to his mother- and father-in-law. There is also a tribute to poetry as a loving woman, and a consideration that the poet, behind melancholy's door, is a 'dreamer of fables'. Summer prevails in *The Home Fire* with poems about its dream and its book, and chosen elements lend a natural background to the intimate portraits: the woman in wine, the power in abundant winds, the ember as wearing in her hair 'the volcano's rose', the fullness of night, and, lastly, the poet himself as coming from, and finding, his own rebirth in the light.

Trazos en un paréntesis ('Sketches in a Parenthesis', 1965–2000, published 2000), as the subtitle – *Poemas no recogidos en libros*, 'Poems Not Included in Books' – indicates, would seem to be a kind of miscellany but the section headings, 'Initial Sonnets', 'A Smile on the Road' and 'Homages and Testimonies', indicate that three aspects of Justo Jorge Padrón's art are offered: the sonnet's agility, the wryness of ironic humour and the sense of admiration and bearing witness, sometimes, even to what is awful and terrifying. The eleven sonnets of the first part start with a welcome to the reader who is invited to listen to a passionate heartbeat paradoxically based on an absence that is a child of the poet's memory and fate. To counter one text about pain, another, with a nod to Shakespeare, calls on temperance to offset the doubt of being. As there is a tribute to the mystery incarnate in trees, Argentine poet and story writer Jorge Luis Borges (1899–1986) is remembered for his revelatory reach for the universe. One sonnet evokes gypsy music, another Padrón's wife Kleo's kiss, another sees the couple as two heartbeats, two bonfires, in their stand facing the world.

The second section of *Sketches in a Parenthesis* deals with humorous characters, often created by the poet, and even with the mockery of self-love. He rails against Mondays and portrays the poet who falls out of favour with the head of a lyric coterie. Some of Padrón's created figures include the captain who scorns success, the man within forever in a hurry, and Rosendo, the little elephant who disappears when the young creator wants to understand the human heart. Others range from the harlequin of wine who strikes sculptural poses to a laughing boy who holds the key to childhood. 'Shoes for Death' recalls Pavese's remark that death will come and have your eyes, but this time it will have, not the rain, as in the last poem of *The Sea's Visit*, but your shoes, guilty of lending man support.

The third section offers evocations of Grand Canary Island, of Lake Ohrid in southern Macedonia and a Greek coastal town, but these gentle scenes give way to brief considerations of death, the presence of the unspeakable, the silence of the unknown and the state of no memory. A tribute to Goya as himself a whirlwind, and a farewell to the twentieth century with its 'genocide weapons' and its denial of existence, comprise a grim ending to a sizeable body of poetry, but they also represent a reflection of Padrón's concern, in his introduction, regarding governments responsible for 'the blind destruction of nature that feeds and protects us'.

LOUIS BOURNE
Madrid, July, 2002

INDEX OF TITLES

Some poetry in translation from Anvil

www.anvilpresspoetry.com